THE COMPLETE FRUGAL LIVING BIBLE

A TO Z

Healthy Minimalist Living with Homesteading

By

David Coleman

&

Joyce Coleman

Published by:

CSB Academy Publishing Company.

P.O. Box 966

Semmes, Alabama 36575

Cover & Interior designed

By

Angie Anderson

First Edition

TABLE OF CONTENTS

INTRODUCTION

My name is David Coleman. I work as an assistant store manager for a national drug store chain. I have been working for this company for the last four years. I married my high school sweetheart, Joyce, and we have three kids. Joyce works from home as a virtual assistant for an online marketing company, but, since our youngest son was born, even with dual income, we have been suffering financially. It all started out with me taking a personal loan to pay for the expense of some unexpected pregnancy-related medical bills that our insurance company didn't cover.

We were never well off by any stretch of the imagination, but I would say we got by okay until two years ago, but lot has changed in the past two years. I found myself not being able to meet the expenses of our basic necessities at times and the frustration of not being able to meet my family obligations drove me crazy.

I even got a part time pizza delivery job, but that didn't help much either. My day job is really not a day job; I work mostly nights as a closing manager. The only days I could deliver pizza were when I was off, or during the day when I wasn't at my primary job, which ended up being only two nights.

During my time at the pizza place, I met a fellow driver, Nathan, who had been working there for 8 years, who told me he too has 3 kids and he lives off the income he has from delivering pizza full time, along with his wife's part-time income, as she works as a front desk clerk at one the local law offices. I broke down and told him how badly I was suffering just to make ends meet and told him I was seriously considering about filing for bankruptcy.

Here is a snapshot of our monthly expenses vs. income back then, just take a look, and you will see we were in the red.

Coleman Family Budget November 2014

Housing	Expenses
Mortgage or rent	$1,160
Phones(2)	$119
Electricity	$187
Gas	$88
Water and sewer	$46
Cable/Internet	$119
Maintenance or repairs	$227
Supplies	$20
Other	$0
Subtotals	$1,966

Transportation

Car Note	$327
Health Insurance	$233
Auto Insurance	$112
Licensing	$0
Fuel	$289
Maintenance	$42
Other	$0
Subtotals	**$1,003**

Food

Groceries	$677
Dining out	$271
Dog Food	$57
Subtotals	**$1,005**

Personal Care

Medical(Co-pay & Prescription)	$78
Hair/nails	$42
Clothing	$77
Dry cleaning	$21
Health club	$0

Organization dues or fees	$0
Movies, games, DVDs	$35
Subtotals	$253

Loans

Personal (Medical Loan)	$766
Credit card - Chase	$144
Credit card - Discover	$187
Credit card - Citi	$100
Other	$0
Subtotals	$1,197

All Total Expenses $5,424

Income

Income David	$3,471.00
Income Joyce	$1,425.00
Total Income:	$4,896.00

Net Savings (Loss) -$528.00

Nathan strongly advised me against filing for bankruptcy, and told me it is not hard to make ends meet as long as I can learn how frugal living works and plan accordingly. He then shared ideas and facts about how he started in a frugal living lifestyle, how the savings accumulate, and how it can truly be a healthy living lifestyle. The conversation was so eye opening that I rushed home and told my wife Joyce all about it and then ended up staying up all night writing down the things he shared. I was anxious to try them all out from the very next day.

Long story short, we started out trying his ideas, one after another. At first, I will admit, it was hard to change some of the old habits, but we were able to do them almost all, as we had no other choice. Nathan was the angel in our life who showed us how we can still have a normal life with the income we have.

I am happy to report that I paid off the loan that I took two years ago. More importantly, after seven years of married life, we finally have a little savings now. Since I paid off the loan, I just set aside the same amount of money, but instead of paying for the loan payment, I just put it in our IRA account.

Finally, we are free! Financial freedom at last! We are happier than ever, and I was told recently that they are looking to promote me as a store manager!!

But this is not about me, but you. Joyce suggested that since we had so much written down as far what we did and how it worked, we should publish a book and share with people like ourselves who are suffering. So here we are.

Don't take my advice with a grain of salt; instead follow them through till you see the results. Remember, you have to stick with them to see results, and remember it is all about the trickle down effect. Not all your savings will come from doing just one thing. Instead, the savings are the very results of many mini changes and adjustments that you will make in your home and daily life.

One more thing; I never went to college, never wrote more than a few pages on anything. This is our first try at writing, and very likely our last as well, so I will ask for your forgiveness ahead of time for any errors or mistakes you may find in our book. Just know that the content is authentic and pure but the delivery method may not be.

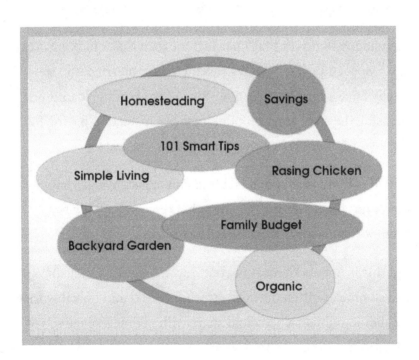

4 MAIN BENEFITS OF FRUGAL LIVING

After going through the suggestions that Nathan made, Joyce and I decided to do a little fact finding a mission, and, with a little research, I started to realize we could cut our spending, save more money and still have a decent life. If you are like me, then let me take a moment to tell you about the four benefits you can enjoy by choosing to live a frugal life and see if that changes your mind.

1. Reduced Stress

If you're reading this book, then it is likely because you have felt the stress and anxiety of wondering where the money is going to come from to pay your bills. You know how stressful this can be, sometimes to the point of making you physically sick. Imagine not having to worry about how you're going to pay all your bills or having the feeling of being able to put some money back into your savings account. I felt this when I started to live frugally.

The American Psychological Association did a study that showed 72% of Americans were stressed over money. Imagine being able to live frugally and not having this stress hanging over you. While this doesn't necessarily mean you won't stress over money at all anymore, it does mean you can be more relaxed and know your basic needs are cared for.

2. More Time for What Matters

Keeping up with the Joneses is a time-consuming process. Whether you are working the majority of your waking hours, or if you are simply spending your time shopping and upgrading what you already own, you aren't left with much free time for what matters. On the other hand, when you live a frugal lifestyle, you don't shop unless you need to, and this leaves you with more time for the more important things in life such as spending time with family, starting a new hobby or just relaxing and enjoying your new stress-free life.

3. Early Retirement

As if the above benefits weren't enough to influence you to make the move to frugal living, consider the fact that with all the money you save you may be able to retire early. This was a major motivating factor for me since I wanted to enjoy my golden years and not spend it slaving for a paycheck.

4. Environmental Benefits

Beyond the basics of saving money and changing your personal life for the better, living frugally can also change the environment around you. When people make fewer purchases and consume less, it can have a positive impact on the environment in a number of ways.

Living frugally taught me how to reuse and re-purpose items rather than throwing them away. This means fewer things are going into landfills, dumps, and waterways. In addition, when you use more used items than new items, you are reducing the amount of product packaging that is made and thrown away in the course of a year. Also, purchasing a more fuel efficient car means you are helping to reduce air pollution and greenhouse gas pollution

Now I won't lie to you, the first month of going frugal is difficult and isn't for everyone. You can't simply start living frugally and save 50% or more per month without a bit of work. You need to do a little bit of work and have discipline in order to start living a frugal lifestyle and enjoying the benefits above.

Today's culture is dominated by a lifestyle centered on spending money. Advertisers are constantly pushing ads that prompt people to buy. Many of these ads focus on basic emotions such as fear, survival, and pleasure. We feel like we're meant to deserve and need what we see in ads. As a result, many find themselves in a financial conundrum where they can't really afford things, but feel they need to have them in order to have a normal lifestyle.

This is something we quickly learned when we started to live frugally. I found out we relied on money for too many things that we didn't really need. I found out we were spending money on things to help with our dissatisfaction over stressful work and buying items that we thought would make us happier. But that was not the case.

While the first month of living frugally was overwhelming and difficult, looking back, I now realize I wouldn't change it for anything. This book is going to help take you through all the stages of living frugally that we learned - groceries, home maintenance, transportation, personal care, entertainment, pet care and more. Hopefully, this will make your transition to frugal living easier, and you can come to see all the benefits that we have enjoyed since making the switch to frugal living. So let's get started.

5 STEPS TO CUT YOUR GROCERY BILL IN HALF

Food is expensive, and prices are going up constantly. The average family spends about 15% of their income on groceries, which means about $9,000 a year. Even as wages stay the same, prices of food continue to increase. This is scary if you are trying to feed a family.

Many have turned to using coupons as a source of saving money on groceries. While these can offer your dramatic savings, they also require a lot of time to find, clip and sort. Instead, I've found there are five other options that can help you cut your grocery bill in half.

1. **Shop Sales**

While it is true that coupons will save you money, the better savings come from store sales. Look for promotions and buy when food is on sale. I'm not talking a few dollars off, but when food is 30-50% off regular price. You can easily go online or look in the local newspaper ads to find the best sales prices. Often, if one store has something on sale another store will try to compete by offering a better deal.

I'm not saying you should buy food just because it's on sale. Rather, always be on the lookout for food you normally buy. Nearly all types of food will go on sale eventually. Never exclude a store simply because it is known to be too expensive. Always check all ads since you might find some stores have cheaper prices on their own brands than a popular brand. Your goal when shopping is to only buy an item when it is at its lowest price possible.

2. Buy in Bulk and Store

In order to be successful in buying only when items are on sale, you need to buy in bulk enough to get by until it goes on sale again. This is the key to saving money on your groceries. Typically an item will go on sale every six to eight weeks, so you will need to buy enough to get by for that long. If you only buy a week's worth at a time, then you may have to pay a higher price to stock up again when you need it.

If you are trying to live frugally, I know it may seem counterintuitive to buy more rather than less. However, if you buy more while items are on sale, then you will be saving on your overall grocery bill. The goal of frugal living is to have your own mini-grocery at home so you can easily plan family meals for cheap.

When I stay stockpile, this doesn't mean you need a basement full of several years worth of food. As I stated before, sale cycles typically occur every six to eight weeks. So you want to have a stockpile that lasts at least this long and provides you with a nice variety of food to choose from. Stockpiling doesn't mean you have to limit yourself to canned and processed foods. There are plenty of options when it comes to stockpiling such as beans, rice, whole grain pasta, whole grain cereals, frozen vegetables and many other products. Plus, later, we will discuss how you can preserve some food options such as meat and dairy products, so you always have plenty of choices on hand. When you do this, you will start to see a dramatic reduction in your grocery bill.

3. Eat Less Meat

A significant portion of a family's grocery bill goes towards meat. So even cutting out a little bit of meat from your grocery list can save you up to $1,000 a year. This doesn't mean you have to become a vegetarian, simply reduce how much meat you eat. When you do purchase meat, stick with the goals in the first two points: buy on sale and buy in bulk.

4. Plan Meals Carefully

In today's busy world, most of us are used to winging it when it comes to meal planning. Think about it; how many times a week do you go to the grocery store for a last minute dinner idea. This step won't be that difficult once you've worked on the above steps. You will no longer need to run to the store for last minute dinner items but instead, go to the stockpile you have at home. This will not only help with reducing your grocery bill, but it will also help you save time shopping and avoid making any impulsive or last minutes buys that impact your budget.

If you are used to buying your food based on what you plan to make, then this step may be a little harder for you. The trick is to get in the habit of planning your meals around the items on sale and the items you already have stockpiled at home. When you reduce the number of non-sale items you buy each week, you will be able to plan your meals in advance and still reduce your grocery bill by half.

5. Match Coupons with Stores

As I stated earlier, coupons can save you money, but they shouldn't be the first item on your list when it comes to cutting your grocery bill in half. After following the four steps above, you are going to see a dramatic reduction in your grocery bill, even without having to use a single coupon. However, you can also use coupons to get even bigger savings on your grocery bill. You need to match coupons to store sales in order to save big. Hold on to your manufacturer's coupons and use them when something goes on sale.

Check your mailbox for coupon mail outs, clip them and organize them by category, this way you don't have to dig through hundreds of coupons to find the one for Hunt's ketchup, etc. Also, there are few great websites where you can go and look for coupons as well, sites like:

https://www.coupons.com

https://www.coolsavings.com/coupons

https://www.grocerycouponnetwork.com/coupons

http://www.couponsurfer.com/grocery/all-grocery

http://www.couponsherpa.com/grocery-coupons/

http://www.valpak.com/coupons/savings/groceries

Don't forget to sign up for any and all rewards program your local grocery, and other stores, offer. This way, any time you are buying fuel to medicine or any such items, you start accumulating reward points which you can redeem at a later date.

Changing your shopping patterns and habits isn't easy and will take some time. However, when you use these simple steps, it will be easier for you and you'll start noticing savings in your grocery bill. Now let's look at how you can reduce your utility bills.

HOW TO REDUCE UTILITY BILLS BY 25%

Before we started to live frugally, our utility bills were easily $200-$500 a month. This was getting really difficult with other costs of living increasing while wages aren't rising nearly as fast. So the next step we took were to consider how to reduce our utility bills by 25%. There are two important areas to focus on in order to save money on your utility bills:

1. What you do around the house and
2. What you do to the house.

Let's look at several things you can do in both of these areas to help reduce your utility bills by at least 25%.

CHANGE WHAT YOU DO AROUND THE HOUSE

These are some simple things that anyone can do in their day to day routines to help make an impact on their utility bills. So the next time you go to do some household chores, consider doing these small things and watch your savings add up at the end of the month.

1. Wash Clothes in Cold Water

A surprising fact we learned is that 90% of the energy a washer uses goes to heating the water. Compound this with the fact that the average American household does about 400 loads of laundry in a year. When you switch to washing clothes in cold water, you will really see the savings add up at the end of the month.

2. Fill the Dishwasher and Avoid Large Dishes

You should never run the dishwasher with a half full load. Make sure you've packed as many dishes as you can before running a wash cycle. Then make sure you turn off the Heat Dry feature and let your dishes air dry for maximum energy efficiency.

Then there are few dishes you should never put in the dishwasher. Large pots, pans, and dishes will take up a lot of room in the dishwasher so you won't be able to clean as much at one time. So these larger items should be washed and dried by hand.

3. Strategically Plan Your Cooking

An oven takes a lot of energy to heat. So if you are going to cook something small, consider using a more energy efficient appliance such as a toaster oven. A toaster oven is also quicker, so it reduces the amount of energy used. Microwaves also take less energy than an oven or stop top. So plan your meal preparation according to the best energy needs.

4. Nightly Electricity Check

Everyone leaves something on while they sleep. Sometimes these are necessary for a comfortable climate, such as fans. However, there are other items that take up energy while we sleep and cost us money. Before you go to bed every night, do a sweep through your house and look for anything you may be able to turn off. For example, just turning off your cable box every night will save you almost $20 a year. See what you can turn off and watch your savings increase.

5. Adjust Hot Water Settings

Heating your water too much not only increases risk of scalding, but it can also cost you a lot in energy bills. The Environmental Protection Agency states that a water heater set at 140 degrees or higher will waste up to $160 a year in standby heat losses in order to keep water at temperature. In order to save money on your energy bill, turn your electric heater off or turn the gas heater down. I looked at my water heater and found that the thermostat was set to 165 degrees, which I changed down to right around 125 degrees and that gave me a savings of around $160 each year.

MAKE CHANGES TO THE HOUSE

In addition, there are a few improvements you can do to your house to increase your energy bill savings. If you rent your home, you may not be able to do some of these. However, most of these are simple and cheap things you can do to improve the energy efficiency of your home and reduce your utility bill.

1. Insulate

Insulation is an important way to prevent energy from escaping your home. According to the US Department of Energy, the majority of a home's heat escapes through the attic and most homes don't have adequate insulation to keep heat inside the home. It is estimated that you can save 20% on your heating and cooling costs by just properly insulating your home. Fiberglass insulation is cheap and very easy to install yourself.

Here is a video I found that was very helpful to us on YouTube:

https://www.youtube.com/How to Insulate Your Attic

Another smaller insulation project to consider is outlets and light switches. Most people don't realize how much air leaks from these areas. Insulation should be added to these areas, especially if they are on an outside wall. Just make sure that when you insulate, you buy a specialized outlet and switch plate seal found at any hardware store.

Lastly, you want to insulate your water heater. You can save 4-9% on water heating costs when you insulate an older water heater. Adding an insulating water heater jacket will allow you to heat water more efficiently.

Here is a video that helped me insulating our water heater, take a look:

https://www.youtube.com/Insulate Your Water Heater

2. Weather Stripping

Weather stripping is another home improvement item you can install yourself for cheap, and it will help to seal drafts in your home. Weather stripping will also keep out rain and prevent inside air from escaping. All of this can have a major impact on your energy bills.

3. Install a Programmable Thermostat

Installing a programmable thermostat will save you 10% on your utility bill. While this is a little more difficult to install, it still isn't that complicated. The thermostat will come with detailed instructions so you should be able to do it on your own.

Once you have it installed, remember that the more you turn it down in winter and the higher you turn it up in the summer, the more you will save on your utility bills. This will take some getting used to, but if you need you can make small adjustments until you get comfortable. A programmable thermostat will help you to reduce your energy bills by setting the temperature in your home and controlling energy use.

4. Install Low-Flow Shower Heads

An older shower head puts out four to five gallons of water a minute. With a low-flow shower head, you are only putting out 1.5 gallons. Honestly, this change only cost us $37 to self-install two low-flow shower heads, and we are now able to save money each day.

5. Energy Star Appliances

Refrigerators, washers, furnaces and water heaters that are Energy star rated will use a fraction of energy compared to non-rated appliances. Often an energy star appliance is priced competitively. In the long run, no matter what you pay for energy star appliances you will get your money back. Next time you have to buy a large appliance look for the Energy Star logo.

6. Paint Your Roof White

This is something you can consider doing if you own your home. A study found that in sunny climates, buildings with white roofs took 40% less energy to cool. This means you would save more than $100 a year. Most hardware stores carry white, elastomeric coating that will work perfectly. This coating is a blend of polymers that is durable, flexible and waterproof so you will not only save on your utility bill, but you will also increase the life of your roof.

7. HVAC Filters

When was the last time you changed the filter on your HVAC system? The longer you wait to change the filter the less efficient your HVAC system becomes and the more it costs you in electricity. The best option is to buy a reusable filter that you can hose off when it becomes clogged. Disposable filters need to be changed every three months, and a reusable filter will recoup these costs in about 15 months. In our house there are two 20x20 AC filters. I went ahead and bought two reusable ones from a local HVAC supply store for $25 each, and now all I do is wash them once every 30-45 days and reuse them. Cool huh?

8. Seal Gaps

Even the smallest of the air leaks in your home will have a big impact on your utility bill. In order to save money, you should use expanding foam or caulking to seal up any cracks. Some common areas to check include the following:

- Windows

- Doorframes

- Rim joist or the top of the basement wall

- Where pipes enter and exit the home

Here is the video I found to be very helpful on sealing gaps. Watch this video where they use an infrared digital reader to show you air leaks and how to fix them.

https://www.youtube.com/sealing doors and windows

Both water and energy use plays a major role in your utility bill. By implementing the steps above, you can have a major impact on your utility bill. While these changes may not seem like much, and some won't even cost you anything; they will give you huge savings on your utility bill. Next, let's consider how to save money on clothing and back to school supplies.

HOW TO CUT CLOTHING AND SCHOOL SUPPLY COSTS BY HALF

I've never been much of a clothes shopper, but at some point in our lives, we all need to buy clothes. Whether we need them for work or we want a new pair of skinny jeans. If you have kids, then you know you have to do this often, as they grow out of their clothes fast. Every time we go clothes shopping I'm amazed at how expensive clothing is becoming. So we decided that in order to completely live a frugal life we also needed to learn how to save money on clothing costs. After doing lot of research on and offline, Joyce came up with few ways we could do it. Consider these four simple ways to reduce your clothing costs.

4 WAYS TO CHEAPER CLOTHING

1. Choosing Where to Shop

When it comes to clothes shopping, I know a lot of people who think the key to saving money is buying when items are on sale or go to a factory outlet store. While this can save you some money, there are a lot of other options where you can go for even better savings and to make your clothing budget go further. Consider instead buying your clothing at secondhand stores such as thrift stores, consignment stores, and garage sales.

Sometimes you may even find a secondhand shop that caters to a specific type of clothing so it will be easier to find what you are looking for. At most of these stores, you can find nice, well-made clothing for a fraction of what you would pay at retail stores. The Goodwill store we have on the west side of the city, usually always carries mostly newer and great quality clothing. We go there at least once every month.

2. Hand Me Downs

Hand me downs don't just have to be for kids. We all have at least several friends, and it is likely that at least one of them is the same size as you. Why not ask if they have clothes they no longer wear? Even if this idea isn't appealing to you, why not consider offering a trade to someone you know. This way you can swap clothes and always have something new to wear without having to pay retail.

3. Focus on Quality Over Price

It may not seem cost effective at first, but sometimes it is better to pay higher for a clothing item. Always consider the long-term and focus on quality over price. For example, you wouldn't want to pay $20 for a shirt you only wear five times before it has to be thrown away when you could pay $100 for a quality shirt that you could wear two hundred or more times. In addition, if your job requires you to buy high-end clothing, you should go for something of quality that costs a little more, but doesn't require you to repurchase clothing as often.

4. Avoid Sales

While shopping the sale is a good idea for groceries, the opposite is true for clothes shopping. Even if you shop during heavily discounted days, this is not the way to live frugally. The reason is that if you shop on a sale day, you may be tempted to buy more. Frugal living is also about simple living. Your closet should have twenty to thirty clothing items that are practical and high quality to be worn many times; not crammed with over two hundred items that you may only wear once. Just remember, you are not trying to save money for next 3-6 months so you can catch on the bills, but think of it as your new lifestyle of simple living.

9 STEPS TO SAVE ON BACK TO SCHOOL SUPPLIES

In addition to clothing, back to school is a one time of the year when you are looking at expensive trips to various stores. PriceGrabber did a recent survey that found 48% of parents would spend $250-$350 or more for each child on back to school supplies. As school budgets dwindle, the costs are passed on to the parents. As your list of school supplies increases, there are nine things you can do to help reduce your cost of back to school supplies.

1. Shop from a List

Before you even leave your home, make sure you have a list from your school of what supplies you are going to need. While most stores may provide one, it is best to get one from your school so you can price shop before you head to the store. Once you have the list in hand, you are ready to start gathering the necessary supplies.

2. Set Limits

When you do go to the store, your kids are undoubtedly going to want something more expensive. While you don't necessarily have to say no, you do want to set some clear limits. Perhaps you can buy the bare minimum and then provide your kids with a set dollar amount, and they can choose what items they want to spend it on from the more expensive items.

3. Check for What You Already Have

Before you head to the store, you want to take a look around your home. You will be surprised at the number of items you still have from last year. Often you can find plenty of notebooks, pencils, crayons, pens, folders and other various supplies to get your kids through a year. Even if you don't have enough, it can reduce the amount you have to buy.

4. Buy in Bulk

When you do go out shopping, if you happen across a good sale on items your kids are likely to need next year then buy in bulk if you can afford it. Pens, pencils, erasers, etc. These are all items you can buy for cheap and stock up to have plenty for next year. This way then the next year you will be able to have more money for the more expensive items on the list. This can be helpful since as your children move up the grade levels, the number of supplies and types of supplies often get more expensive; so you should start saving up now.

5. Visit the Dollar Store

There are quite a few school supplies that you can find at a dollar store for cheap. While you won't be able to get everything on your list at the dollar store, quite a few smaller items are there. This way you can get a good price and have a little more left over to spend on the bigger items.

6. Tax-Free Weekends

A lot of states have tax-free weekends during the back to school time of year. During this time retailers often offer big sales and, with a little smart shopping, you can take advantage of them.

7. Store Specific Savings

You can get extra savings through discount or loyalty programs offered by some stores. For school clothing and shoes, a lot of stores also offer web-based coupons. When you pair these discounts with store sales, you will save a lot of money on your school supplies.

8. Don't Upgrade

At one time, parents didn't have to worry about gadgets until a child reached the upper grades of school or college. Now, gadgets are important for kids of all age and grade levels. When it comes to purchasing electronics you want to resist the urge to upgrade. While all the stores are trying to get you to buy the newest digital gadgets in September, your best option is to buy last year's model. Often these go on sale in September for a decent price. If your child wants an upgraded model, then have them save up for it during the summer to give them valuable financial tools.

9. Shop Refurbished

Lastly, if you are going to buy the newest and latest electronics, then you should consider buying refurbished. Refurbished electronics often sell for 15 to 20% less. A number of online stores including EBay and other similar sites, along with some local retail stores, have areas where you can get refurbished devices and save a lot of money.

Next, let us discuss how you can save money on fuel for your car.

HOW TO SAVE ON FUEL COSTS

Every time I wake up in the morning, it seems like the cost of gas has gone up again. The average price of gas is around $3.00 a gallon. With no sign that gas prices are going to be coming down, you need to learn to save money on fuel costs. We all know the basics of fuel consumption, but there is actually quite a bit that you can do to save money on fuel costs. There are four main areas where you can reduce your fuel costs: buying gas, driving smart, maintaining a good car and buying a more fuel efficient option. Let's look at each of these areas individually and what you can do to save on the cost of fuel.

BUYING GAS

1. Save Money with Discount and Rewards Cards

There are several websites, with the most notable being PlasticJungle.com and GiftCardGranny.com, that allow you to purchase discounted gas gift cards. This means you can often get about $100 worth of gas for $95. $5 may not seem like that much of savings, but it can add up over time.

If you find yourself filling up often, then maybe you should consider a credit card that rewards you for buying gas. However, you want to make sure you pay off your balance in full each month, so you don't get affected by the high-interest rates. Another option is the gas rewards programs through grocery stores such as Safeway, Kroger, and Winn-Dixie. This can be a good option, especially if you have a large family that buys a lot of groceries. It is important that you weigh the cost of the gas to the rewards in order to make sure you are saving money.

2. Use Your Smartphone

An excellent way to save money on gas is to use your smartphone. Sometimes you will be able to save up to $0.20 per gallon. There are several apps that you can use. Consider some of the best ones and see which are available on your phone.

GasBuddy is perhaps the most popular. It will help you locate the least expensive gas station as well as the closest option. A good community of users provides you with the latest gas price updates.

If you have an iPhone, there are several apps you can choose from. All of these apps will cost you about $3.00, but they can save you a lot of money at the pump. Your choices include Fuel Finder, AroundMe, Gas Cubby and SmartFuel.

3. When to Get Your Gas

If possible, you should try to fill up your tank on Wednesdays or Thursdays before 10 am. This is because gas prices often increase on Thursday before weekend travel and the majority of gas station owners make their price changes for the day at 10 am. The worst time to buy gas is on Friday, Saturday or Sunday. You also want to buy gas when it is cooler since it will be more dense. When the temperature rises, gas becomes less dense, and you won't get as much.

It is best to fill up when your tank is a quarter full. When you do this, you are extending the gas mileage since you have a lighter fuel load. It also gives you time to buy gas at a bargain. However, if the weather is cold, then you run the risk of condensation. If you run your car with less than a quarter tank you are shortening the life of the electric fuel pump and running the risk of being forced to buy gas wherever you find it, no matter what the price.

4. Where to Get Gas

You should never purchase your gas near a highway; these are usually going to be higher in price. If possible, you want to drive farther away from a highway in order to find cheaper stations. If you happen to live or are traveling near state lines, these are the best places to get gas. Sometimes by crossing into another state where tax rates are different you can save quite a bit on gas.

5. How to Fill Your Tank

The first thing to do is determine how you are going to pay for your gas. A lot of stations charge a premium if you pay with credit cards in order to offset the processing fees that credit card companies charge them. If you can, pay with cash or debit, so you can save some money.

If you only fill your tank halfway, you will be able to reduce your car's weight and increase your mileage slightly. However, if there isn't a cheap gas station on your daily route, this may not be the best option. Although you should never top off your tank when you fill up at the pump. This forces liquid fuel into the evaporative emissions system and can overwhelm the circuits that route fuel tank vapors to the engine.

1. Drive Less

With the rising costs of gas, the obvious solution is to avoid driving if at all possible. For work, look into carpooling as an option. If you're just doing some errands, then consider combining multiple errands into one trip and plan them out, so you don't spend time driving back and forth across town. If you only need to do something nearby maybe you can walk or bicycle. There are plenty of ways in which you can drive less and save money on gas.

2. Plan Your Trips

If you must drive, then you should carefully plan your trips in advance in order to prevent wasting fuel and time. Have a few alternative routes in mind in case your primary route doesn't work. Often planning to take a back road can prevent you from stopping at lights and sitting in traffic jams. Therefore, you should schedule your trips and errands for times when traffic is lighter. If you aren't good with maps, then consider using a GPS system to help you find the fastest and shortest route to your destination.

3. Idling

If you idle your car engine for over a minute, you are wasting fuel and pumping greenhouse gas emissions into the air. Modern car engines don't require an extensive length of time to warm up the engine. Therefore, if you need to warm your car up, don't do it for any longer than 30 seconds. If you're going to be waiting somewhere for a long period of time then turn the engine off rather than idling and wasting gas.

4. Safe Driving

If you drive fast, you are increasing drag and also fuel consumption. Try to drive just below the speed limit and drive smoothly in order to use gas more efficiently. You also want to maintain a safe following distance. If you follow too close to the vehicle in front of you, then you are going to be braking and accelerating more in order to maintain the narrow gap. When you maintain a safe following distance, it is not only safer, but it also gives you more time to work with traffic signals in order to use gas efficiently.

5. Avoid Stops

When you approach a red light, try to slow down enough to avoid having to actually stop. Speeding up from a slow speed is easier on your gas than getting started from a complete stop.

If you travel the same route often enough you can start to anticipate stop signs and lights. You can start to time the lights and maintain the appropriate speed in order to hit all green lights.

If you do have to stop, be sure to take off slowly. This will have a dramatic effect on your gas mileage.

At the same time, you want to monitor how you brake. Excessive braking will waste gas and wear out your brake pads more quickly. Rather maintain a safe following distance when you are in heavy traffic so you won't have to brake as often. With a larger distance between you and the vehicle in front of you, you can also brake earlier when coming up to a traffic light.

6. Reduce Wind Resistance

Just having an open window will increase drag and cost you extra fuel. So whenever possible, keep your windows closed. Also, if you have a rack or carrier on the top of your car, you should take it off when not in use to make your vehicle more aerodynamic.

7. Air Conditioning Use

Everyone loves air conditioning in the summer, but it can also waste a lot of gas. Turn off your AC as much as possible. Consider other options to keep your car cooler, such as parking in the shade or rolling the windows down to circulate air when you're not moving or when traveling at slower speeds. While open windows will increase drag and reduce fuel efficiency, at low speeds running the air conditioning is worse. If the air outside is cool then simply turn on the vent.

CAR MAINTENANCE

In addition to saving money when buying gas and conserving gas by driving smart, you can also follow some simple maintenance tips in order to increase the gas efficiency of your vehicle.

1. Monitor Tire Pressure

Under inflated tires not only causes them to wear out faster, but also wastes gas. Maintaining properly inflated tires will reduce friction and give you better gas mileage. Tire pressures fluctuate due to temperature changes so you should regularly check the psi, especially during seasons with drastic weather shifts. Every few weeks, top off the air in the tires to the manufacturer's recommended pressure. It is best to add air when the tires are cold or driven no more than a mile or so. Filling the tires while they are hot can cause excessive pressure. Excessive pressure can cause bad handling and uneven tire wear.

2. Tune the Engine

You need to regularly tune your car engine. This will allow the vehicle to use less gas. If you can't remember the last time your vehicle had a tune-up, then you should probably schedule one.

3. Change Filters

Regularly check your car's air filters, especially if you live in a dusty area. When your filters are clean, the car will run more efficiently.

4. Proper Motor Oil

Only use the proper motor oil for your vehicle. If you don't know which type your car requires, then check the owner's manual or look online. When you use the wrong motor oil, the engine will need to work harder and in turn burn more fuel.

5. Change Spark Plugs

Even the highest level of platinum spark plugs that claim to last 100,000 miles will often start having trouble around 75,000 miles. Spark plugs don't cost that much, and. depending on your vehicle can be easy to replace. Be sure to change your spark plugs often to increase the efficiency of your vehicle.

FUEL EFFICIENT VEHICLE OPTIONS

If you happen to be in the market for a new vehicle or can afford to get a new vehicle, then consider a more fuel efficient option to help you live frugally. There are specific types of vehicles you can purchase, or you can still go with a traditional vehicle, but look for a few features that make it more fuel efficient. One car we are about to buy is a Toyota Prius; it is a hybrid with a very good reliability record, and we decided to buy a two year old one, this way we are not paying the MSRP instead we are getting it for almost 25% cheaper than what it cost new.

1. **Manual vs. Automatic**

A manual transmission is going to be more fuel efficient than an automatic transmission. With a manual transmission, you can shift up early and down late in order to save on fuel. You can also shift into neutral when idling to reduce strain on the transmission.

2. **Torque vs. Horsepower**

When choosing a vehicle, focus more on torque specification than horsepower. Most engines produce maximum torque at a rarely used RPM. A maximum torque in the range of 2200 to 3000 RPM will yield usable power. Engines that operate at peak torque will be more efficient.

3. Fuel Efficient Vehicles

There are plenty of options when it comes to fuel efficient vehicles. There are even several models of affordable non-hybrids that get 40 miles per gallon to help you save money on gas.

Then there are hybrids that help offer you immediate savings at the pump. In addition, in the US you can get local state tax breaks when buying a hybrid car. Sometimes a federal deduction of up to $2,000 can be received when you buy a hybrid. Although, you should check with your insurance company first since most hybrids come with higher insurance rates.

There is also the option of buying a diesel. Some of these cars have mileage similar to hybrids. A diesel car also gives you the option of using bio-diesel fuel or waste vegetable oil. However, you should research carefully since diesel fuel may not always be cheaper than regular gas.

Lastly, there is the option of buying a motorcycle or scooter. These are often cheaper and get 70 miles per gallon or more. Again, you need to research carefully to make sure these are the best options for your needs.

Let's take a break from discussing shopping strategies to look at some things you can do around the home to help you live frugally. Homesteading is a popular trend these days, and you can learn a thing or two from these individuals on how to make your dollar stretch further.

HOW HOMESTEADING BASICS CAN HELP YOU LIVE HEALTHY AND SAVE MONEY

Homesteading is a new trend that many are finding has a lot of healthy living and financial benefits. You don't have to go live out in the woods to be a homesteader; there are plenty of things you can do even if you live in an apartment that can help you to live a healthy and frugal lifestyle. First, let's consider twelve ways we have been able to save money and have a frugal lifestyle by using homesteading basics.

12 FINANCIAL BENEFITS OF HOMESTEADING

1. You never have to pay for a gym membership because you have a continuous list of physical tasks to keep you active.

2. For those that own their own home, you can save money on your monthly electricity bill by using your fireplace for heating.

3. If you have the room, you can set up a clothesline to dry your clothes and save a large amount of electricity compared to running your dryer.

4. Cooking meals from scratch can save you a lot of money on food and food preparation.

5. You can grow your own organic produce for a lot less than purchasing it in a store.

6. Along the same lines, preserving your own food saves you money over having to go to the grocery store more often.

7. Bulk fruit can be dried as a good snack food and, again. save you money on your grocery bill and extend the life of your fruit.

8. One grocery item that has increased in cost recently is eggs. If you have room for backyard chickens, you can save money on eggs while also having true organic non-GMO eggs.

9. You save money on medical bills when you are active and eating healthy to have a good lifestyle.

10. You can also save money on over-the-counter medications by growing and drying a variety of herbs to use for home treatments of minor ailments.

11. As you spend more time working around the home, you don't need to spend money eating out at restaurants.

12. Lastly, when you stay around the home and find ways to live frugally you don't need to go out and pay for entertainment.

Now that we have considered the ways homesteading basics can help you save money and improve your life, let's consider just what you can do around your home. The following are eight homesteading basics that I included into my everyday life in order to enjoy the twelve benefits listed above.

1. Grow Your Own Food

Homesteaders become experts at growing their own food, whether it is fruits, vegetables, nuts, meat, fish, eggs, dairy, or herbs. When you grow your own food, you will save money on both food and fuel, because you won't need to go shopping as often. Later, we'll discuss some ways that you can start simple with a garden and some chickens.

2. Food Storage

In addition to growing their own food, homesteaders learn to preserve what they don't eat right away and store up for future use. Take a moment to think about how often you go out to eat because you don't want to cook or how much food you throw away because it goes bad. This can be quite a cost for those trying to live frugally. As we will discuss later, consider preserving your food and storing it up for future use.

3. Reuse Items

There are a number of ways to reuse items. For example, I use the large bulk laundry detergent tubs to store my dried foods, flour, sugar, etc. The goal is to never throw out anything you can reuse. This way you can avoid buying items you already have around your house.

4. Wait to Make Purchases

The true key to frugal living is to never owe money. Rather than buying something on credit and having to pay interest, consider waiting to make a purchase and saving up the cash needed. You would be surprised how much you don't really need certain items right away, and sometimes you may find out you don't even need it by the time you save up the money for it.

5. The Library is a Resource

There are plenty of ways you can use the library as a frugal living resource. First, just consider books. How many books in your home have you actually read? Multiply the number of books in your home by the cost of an average book. If you had gone to the library for those books rather than purchasing them, you would save a lot of money. You can also use the library for DVD movies. That can save you a lot of money on movie rentals. Lastly, you can use the library as an internet source if you don't want to pay for it at home and save on your utility and electric bill.

6. Use It Up

Another important part of living frugally is to never purchase something until you absolutely need it. If you buy clothes, wear them until they are completely worn out and not suitable for use anymore. Don't just toss bottles when they get low, wait until you absolutely can't get anything more out of them.

7. Be Content

Don't make a purchase unless you are sure you really need it. Advertisements are designed to make us feel like we must have items that we don't really need. Often you can be content with what you have and save a lot of money in the process. If you need, make a list of what you feel you must have and a list of what you need to be content and happy. You'll be surprised just what you can live without.

8. Set Priorities

It seems the days are getting shorter, and the list of things to get done are getting longer. It is always tempting to start new projects, and we all have grand plans for what we want to accomplish. However, you will soon find yourself wasting money on unfinished projects that you can't use. So take the time to determine what's the most important and finish those projects first before going on to the next one. This will save you both time and money.

Now that we've looked at some of the basics of homesteading and how it can benefit you, I want to take the time to discuss a few more of the basics in detail with you. Let's see how you can have a frugal lifestyle by taking charge of your food.

HOW TO SAVE MONEY ON FOOD

When we first started to live frugally, I thought we were doing good, saving money on my monthly grocery bill. Then a friend of mine introduced me to homesteading basics, and we learned that you could go so much further than just saving money on groceries. We started looking into the actual food we were eating and realized we could also save money by making smart food choices, preparing the smart way, preserving what we didn't need right away, and growing our own food. Let me share with you what we learned and saw how it could help you to live a frugal life.

EATING WELL FOR LESS

1. Make the Smart Choices

Stick to a grocery list. Go to the store prepared, and you are less likely to make impulse purchases. When you arrive at the store, stay to the perimeter. The perimeter of most grocery stores has the healthy whole foods such as fresh produce and meat. When you stick to this perimeter, you are less likely to buy junk food.

Cut out the junk food. Avoid foods like soda, cookies, crackers, prepackaged meals, instant mashed potatoes, white bread, canned soups, refined pasta and sugary cereals. These may seem cheap at first, but they will cost you in the long run both financially and in physical health. Many of these prepackaged and processed foods have high levels of hidden sugar. They fill you up for cheap, but in the end, they cause rapid swings in energy and blood sugar which leads to health problems.

For this reason, it is important to know the good carbs from the bad carbs. Good carbs include whole grains, beans, fruits, and vegetables. These are digested slowly and provide you with long-lasting energy to get through the day. Bad carbs include white flour, refined sugar and white rice that don't have bran, fiber, and nutrients. These carbs digest quickly and only cause short-lived energy.

Even when you are trying to live frugally and eat cheap, you want to make sure you take the time to consider the quality of the food you are purchasing. When you buy high-quality food, you are reducing your exposure to pesticides and antibiotics while increasing the nutritional value of your food.

You can also do this through your meat purchases. Rather than buying expensive cuts of steak from an industrially raised animal, you can often get a cheaper cut from an animal that is organic/grass-fed/free-range.

It pays to educate yourself since some fruits and vegetables have more chemical residue than others. The general rule to follow is that if you are going to eat the skin you want to choose organic, while conventionally grown produce is fine for anything you are going to peel.

2. Protein Options

Protein is something your body relies on for many of its functions. You can get protein from a variety of sources aside from meat. With a few dietary adjustments, you can live frugally and still get plenty of healthy protein options.

In addition to getting a less expensive cut of meat, consider ways you can make it go further. Use your meat to make casseroles, sauces, soups, stews, and stir-fries. Not only can these be easily preserved for future meals, but it also means your money stretches further. You can even use bones for the bone broth that you can add to vegetables, beans, and whole grains to get a wonderfully satisfying meal.

Perhaps meat isn't your thing; then consider some vegetarian sources of protein. Beans and lentils are an inexpensive and tasty option to prepare, plus they store well. Consider stocking your pantry with dried and/or canned beans, lentils, nuts, and seeds.

You can get a good source of both protein and calcium in yogurt, soft cheeses, and kefir. Most of these also contain probiotics that can help improve digestion and mental health. Some non-dairy options include sauerkraut; vegetables pickled in brine, miso soup, and tempeh.

Lastly, a cheap and preservable option is canned fish and chicken. You can easily add these to sandwiches, enchiladas, casseroles, and salads.

3.   Buy in Bulk

When you buy in bulk, you are saving both on time and money. Anything non-perishable such as dried goods and canned goods can be purchased in bulk. Some perishable items can be frozen to last longer, such as meat and bread.

Produce will be cheapest when it is in season; this is also when it is most nutritious. At this time you can often find produce such as apples, oranges, grapefruit, potatoes and onions by the bag for a cheap price. This is a good time to buy in bulk.

If you can't get a good deal on fresh vegetables, then take a look at the frozen foods isle. You can often get a large back of frozen vegetables that are just as nutritious and can allow you to buy in bulk for cheaper.

Anytime you purchase grains it is very easy to do so in bulk. Whether it is whole grain brown rice, millet, barley, rolled oats or even cereal, you can buy in bulk and store in airtight containers to save you money.

Lastly, there is meat. Often meat can be purchased in larger packages for a discounted per pound price. You can split these packages up into meal sized portions and freeze them until you use them.

4. Desserts

I know I stated earlier that you should cut out junk food, and now I'm discussing desserts. The truth is that cutting out sugary junk food doesn't mean you have to get rid of dessert entirely. There are plenty of good dessert options out there that don't include cakes, cookies, and muffins. Consider some frugal and healthy options.

A great option for a hot day is to freeze your own fruit juice into a Popsicle.

For winter months, you can heat the home by making some home baked goods. Oatmeal cookies from rolled oats are a healthy option.

Buy a bulk container of plain yogurt and flavor it with seasonal fruit for a unique dessert option.

If you are going to eat junk food, make it dark chocolate. This is good when you get the craving for sweets since it is high in antioxidants and can be good for you in small amounts.

These are just a few ways you can eat for cheap. However, one area that I find often gets overlooked is the pets. I have a few animals and let me tell you, pet food isn't cheap. So how can you also feed your furry, four-legged family members on a frugal budget? Let's look at a few ways.

9 WAYS TO SAVE ON PET FOOD

1. Buy Online

You can often find a lot of great deals for pet food online. Whether it is a site such as Wag.com or Coupaw.com where you can get discounted pet food or sites like PetSmart and Petco where you can get sales and coupons to save you a lot of money. Many of these websites also offer free shipping deals which can be a great savings when you're shipping a heavy bag of pet food.

2. Generic Food

Just because the food is generic doesn't mean it is low quality. Always check the ingredients, and you'll be surprised that sometimes you can find a decent quality, generic food that is a lot cheaper than a brand name product. Whether it is human products or pet products, it always pays to shop around for the best deal.

3. Subscription Services

Your pet is likely going to be eating the same thing every month so why not sign up for a recurring order. Most websites will give you a product discount when you sign up for repeat delivery. In addition, it will be saving you time and gas when you don't have to travel to a pet store every week or month.

4. Buy in Bulk

If you have a membership at a warehouse store, you can often find pet food in bulk for a lower price. If you can buy food and treats by the pound you are going to save a lot in the long-run and pet food is something that can be stored for longer periods of time.

5. Look for Free Samples

It may take a little time out of your day, but do a daily search for free pet food. A lot of companies regularly offer free samples and sometimes even full-sized products in order to attract customers. You may not be able to feed your animal long term with this option, but it can get you through the financially tight months.

6. Portion Control

The recommendations on a bag of kibble for serving size is often more than a pet needs. Often these recommendations are based on an ideal situation where an animal is outdoors and unaltered. For an indoor, altered pet with a sedentary lifestyle, you can often feed them much less. When you feed according to proper portions, you will be surprised at how far that bag of pet food goes and how much you can save at the end of the month.

7. Make Your Own Treats

There are countless recipes for pet treats online. This can also be a great option if your pet has digestive issues since you can be selective about what you put in their food. In addition, talk to your veterinarian about some people food options that are healthy for your pet so you can give them table scraps as treats and not waste anything.

8. Talk to the Humane Society

If you go on the Humane Society's website, you will find a section for those having trouble affording a pet. This resource will give you countless links to local and national groups that can provide free pet food, discounted vet care, and other cost saving options. Although this list is constantly changing, so if you don't find something in your area, don't give up and keep looking.

9. Food Banks and Food Stamps

If you go on the Petco website, you will find a link to regional groups that distribute food to those who need it. Also, some programs such as Meals on Wheels in certain areas will provide free food to seniors with animals. Then there is a nonprofit group called Pet Food Stamps that provides pet food to those receiving food stamps, welfare, Social Security or other forms of income assistance.

Now that we have looked at the actual food let's get into discussing how food preparation can be done frugally. There are plenty of ways to stretch your money when preparing food.

FRUGAL COOKING

You can save both time and money when you prepare large portions of food for use over multiple meals. There are several ways to do this.

First, you can cook one large meal at the start of the week and then have extra to use later in the week.

Second, you can cook a one-pot dish such as soup, stew or casserole to reduce your preparation time and money. After cooking one dish, you can heat up the leftovers each day after and maybe just add an extra ingredient or two to change it up and keep it unique.

There are a variety of dishes that can help you have some good leftovers. Soups, stews, and stir-fries are a great winter option, and you can always add a sauce or other herbs for a unique flavor each time. You can also use leftovers ingredients to make a burrito. Nearly anything can be put into a tortilla, topped with some salsa and cheese to make an excellent meal. You will be surprised by how many foods and flavors combine together well for another meal.

If you're like us, we didn't like the idea of eating the same thing every day for a week. However, I learned to make our meals more appealing by changing the appearance every time. Depending on the mood I found I could present the same food as a romantic, fun or tasty alternative. Add some color to your meal. Use some tomatoes or carrots to add to a salad. Add some herbs or corn to a soup or stew. In order to truly live frugally and save money you also need to learn how to batch cook.

BATCH COOKING

Batch cooking is the key to frugal living and cooking. Not only does it save you money, but it also saves time for those who are busy working during the week. When you come home tired, you won't need to cook a fancy meal.

Cooking in advance with batch cooking will reduce your shopping bill and save you valuable preparation time. You won't have to worry about wasting food. Batch cooking is also a healthy option since you will be able to avoid the temptation of eating out when you're short on time and too tired to cook a meal from scratch.

There are a few methods of batch cooking, but they all focus on cooking in advance and freezing or stockpiling the leftover food for those times when you don't want to cook. Let's look at the various methods you can use.

You can use this option for entire family meals or for individual dishes. You can cook the meals in advance and then freeze them out for when you want to thaw and reheat a meal. Freezer meals are great for those who don't want to do a lot of cooking or preparation. If you store these in ziplock bags rather than Tupperware, you'll have more room in the freezer. There are plenty of recipes to choose from that taste great when reheated, but some ideas to get you started are the following:

- Chicken nuggets

- Macaroni and cheese

- Beef casserole

- Lamb Stew

- Lasagna

INDIVIDUAL INGREDIENTS

If you don't want to serve up a freezer meal every night, then you can consider preparing individual ingredients in advance and freezing them. You can then make these ingredients into a meal later without having a lot of prep time involved. This means you can make up sauces in advance for adding to a variety of meals. Or you can cook meat or chicken in advance and chop them up into pieces to be added to a variety of dishes at meal time.

Soup

Soup is a very quick dinner that works for a batch cooking option. While canned can be an option, it doesn't have the same taste as homemade. When you batch cook soup, you can store individual meal proportions in the freezer for those times when you want a quick and simple lunch or dinner.

Advanced Cooking

Batch cooking can be done for as many days in advance as you want. Most people find it best to cook one day a week and then preserve the meals for the rest of the week. This way you have plenty of free time on your work days, plus you can still enjoy a little time off when you aren't working.

However, if you have a detailed meal plan and room in your refrigerator or freezer, then you can consider batch cooking for a few weeks to a month in advance. This is a large task and will often take a whole day, but imagine the time and money you can save by only cooking one day a month.

Even with all this care and preparation, there are going to be times when you need to eat out at a restaurant. Or perhaps you just prefer to eat out rather than prepare food at home. No matter what your reason, if you are going to eat out, let us discuss some tips that can help you save some money.

10 WAYS TO BE FRUGAL WHEN EATING OUT

In all our research about frugal living, the common advice was to avoid eating out at restaurants. While it is true you are paying a lot of money to have a meal cooked and prepared for you, it is possible to eat out for cheap. If you're like us, there are going to be times when you just feel like going out to eat, or maybe you have a special occasion to celebrate and want to splurge on eating out at a restaurant. The good news is, this is possible even while living frugally. Let's consider ten ways I've learned to be frugal when eating out at a restaurant.

1. Where to Eat

A fine dining restaurant is going to cost you at least $20 an entree. After salad or soup, wine, dessert and coffee, tax and tip you can easily expect to pay about $50 a person for just one meal. At a casual restaurant, the cost can be a bit cheaper around $10 to $15 a person. However, if you want to save a lot of money, then you should consider a restaurant where you are your own server. When a restaurant doesn't have to pay for wait staff, then they can charge less for food that tastes just as good as a casual chain restaurant. There are several types of restaurants to choose from in this category.

Buffet-style restaurants are an excellent option for families or individuals who plan to eat a large amount of food. You often pay a flat price and have no limit to how much you can eat. Common buffet chains such as Hometown Buffet and Old Country Buffet typically charge about $12 a person.

Fast casual restaurants give you the best of both: a fast food restaurant and a full-service fine dining experience. With this choice you order at a counter, pay the cashier and then pick up your food at the end of the counter. Common chains in this category such as Panera Bread and Chipotle Mexican Grill are about $7 to $10 a meal.

Lastly, there are quick serve restaurants. These are places where you order your food at a counter and get it immediately. This isn't the same as fast food restaurants, but they are the cheapest place to eat where a typical meal costs about $6 a person.

2. Takeout

Another way to save is to eat at home. When you order takeout, you will be saving money on the tip and any drinks or sides that you would order at the restaurant. You can easily order online and then just stop by to pick up your food.

3. Make It a Lunch

If you simply want to eat out on occasion to take a break, then consider eating a lunch meal out since it will be significantly less than eating a dinner. Some restaurants that offer great lunch deals, including Applebee's, Cheesecake Factory, Olive Garden and Red Lobster.

You don't necessarily have to eat in the midday to get these deals either. Most restaurants are extending their lunch hours into late afternoon. So if you're willing to eat dinner a little early, then you may be able to get it for the cost of a lunch time meal.

4. Eat Out on Your Birthday

This may only be once a year, but if you only eat out on special occasions, then this should be one of them. Most websites have a birthday or anniversary club that you can sign up for online.

Then as your birthday approaches, these restaurants will often give you a free drink or dessert, and some will even give you a free entree.

5. Split a Meal

Most restaurants serve you way more than a typical serving size. That means that if you eat the entire meal, you are overeating. On the other hand, if you leave half of your food on the plate you're being wasteful. Either way, you are paying more for a meal than you need to.

One thing you can choose to do is split the meal with someone. Some restaurants will allow you to ask for the main course and an extra plate so you can divide the meal when it comes. Sometimes you may be charged an extra plate fee, but this is often only a dollar or two. Another option is for one individual to order a small side such as a soup or salad while the other orders the entree and then split both when they come. This not only saves you money, but is also good for your diet as well since you are eating a proper serving size.

6. Take Home Leftovers

If you don't have someone to split the meal with then, you can consider splitting the meal into two for yourself. Rather than eating everything, stop when you're full and take home the leftovers as a second meal. This way you can get two meals for the price of one. If you have trouble disciplining yourself to eat only a single serving, then you can ask the server to bring a to-go container at the start of the meal. This way you can put aside half of the food before you start eating.

7. Avoid Drinks

While food is expensive at restaurants, the markup on drinks is even higher. This includes both alcoholic and non-alcoholic drinks. So when you go out to eat, it is a good idea to skip the drinks entirely and just drink water with your meal. If you must have a drink with your meal, look for restaurants that allow you to bring your own bottle and only charge a modest corkage fee.

8. Have a Special Meal

While ordering the cheapest meal that you like on the menu may seem like the best option; this may not always be the case. You don't want to pay a high price, even if it is the cheapest on the menu, for something you can make for cheaper at home. Rather look at as more from the point of view of how much money you are throwing away eating the dish at a restaurant rather than making it at home. For example, the pasta dish may be only $12, but you may be able to make it at home for only a few dollars. Versus the meal that costs $22 but you either can't make it at home or all the ingredients together costs you about the same. So if you're going to eat out at a restaurant, order something you won't be able to make at home.

9. Discounts

There are plenty of ways to lower the cost of your meal out through discounts and coupons. Consider some of the more popular options that can help you save some money.

Restaurant.com offer discounted gift certificates for many restaurants in order to increase customers. For example, you can get $25 worth of food for only $10. However, you want to carefully consider the restrictions to make sure you are actually getting a good deal.

Entertainment books are another great option. You can often find one for your area, and it will include coupons for restaurants and attractions. There is a subscription fee for these books, but you can often get savings of up to 50% so you can usually get your money back pretty quickly.

Group deals on websites such as Groupon or LivingSocial is another great option. When you buy deals through these websites, you can often save 50% or more. Again, just make sure you read the terms carefully before signing up for a deal and pay attention to the expiration dates.

Most people tend to throw away the coupons packs that come in the mail, but you may want to think twice. Valpak and SmartSource are two sets of coupons that often come through the local newspaper or directly to your mailbox. Both of these options can provide you with some good coupons to local eateries.

If there is a local eatery you like, consider checking out their Facebook page or websites. Most local businesses will offer deals or weekly specials. If you subscribe to their online newsletters sometimes you may even get special discounts.

The important thing to remember is that even though you are using a coupon, always calculate your tip based on the original amount of the bill. Your server is still doing a lot of work whether you are paying the full price or not. Plus if you are saving money off your meal it is only fair you use some of that savings to provide a generous tip for your server.

10. Cash Back

There is also a way to save money even after you've gone out to eat. If you chose to pay with a cash back credit card, then you can get 1-5% of your money back. Now if you're trying to live frugally, you don't necessarily want to put everything on credit cards. However, if you budget and pay off your credit cards at the end of the month without any interest being added then why not use them to get a little cash back.

Restaurant meals are going to cost you more than a budgeted, home cooked meal. However, if you are living a frugal lifestyle, you don't want to eat out every night. Although the occasion splurge isn't the bad, especially if you use some of the tips above to help you save some money. For those who really want to live frugally then you will want to do everything at home, including growing your own food. Let's take a look at how you can start a backyard garden to grow your own fruits and vegetables.

BACKYARD GARDENING

I've never had a green thumb. I can't grow anything. So when Nathan told me the best way to frugal living was growing my own food, I was a little concerned. If living frugally meant growing my own food, I was going to starve. However, after a little research and help from Joyce, I started to realize that growing vegetables is actually easy. With a little knowledge and effort, we have been able to grow decent vegetables. Let's discuss some of the things we learned to help you get started with your backyard gardening.

PLANNING A VEGETABLE GARDEN

Growing vegetables is a bit different from other forms of gardening. The majority of vegetables are annuals, so you need to start from scratch every year. Throughout the season you often find yourself re-planting.

When it comes to planning a vegetable garden it all comes down to design. Designing a vegetable garden isn't about looks, rather it is more about which vegetables grow better near each other. Some vegetables excrete substances that prevent other plants from growing. Tall vegetables can shade other vegetables that need sunlight. Vegetables that are in the same family will attract similar pests so they should be moved each year.

However, the good news is that once you design your vegetable garden, the majority of the hard work is done. Most vegetables have the same growing requirements, so after designing and planting, there are just a few general guidelines to follow. We found a few great YouTube videos that were very helpful, but I didn't want to include any links of those because as I went back to find those videos, most were gone. So just do a search, and you will find many videos that can guide you through this planning.

CONSIDERATIONS BEFORE PLANTING

Sun

Most vegetables like the sun and grow their best with six to eight hours of direct sunlight. Leafy greens can grow with less sun and crops that prefer cool weather such as lettuce will grow well in the summer if shaded by taller plants. However, you still want to choose a full sun location when planting a vegetable garden.

Access

You want your vegetable garden to be close to a water source and as close to your kitchen as possible. Vegetables need to be watered on a regular schedule. If you water them too erratically, they will develop problems such as cracking open, not setting any fruit or becoming prone to cultural problems. To help with regular watering, you want them to be easily accessible from the house.

Soil

For any garden, soil is the most important factor. Annual vegetables spend their entire season producing flowers and fruits, so the soil is very important. Vegetables are heavy feeders, and a rich soil will keep them growing while helping them ward off disease and pest problems.

To start, you want a soil that is rich in organic matter. You'll need to replenish the organic matter every year. You can add compost and composted manure in spring and/or fall. It is also a good idea to have the soil tested whenever you start a new garden. These test results will tell you if any other amendments are needed to the soil or if the pH needs to be adjusted.

I found the best way to ensure good soil for my vegetable garden was to create raised beds. This means the soil you are growing in is higher than the ground by six or more inches. This allows you to control the soil in the planting area, prevent it from getting stepped on and compacted; it drains well, and it will warm up faster in the spring, so planting is easier.

Lastly, when considering soil you want to be aware of run-off and drainage. Vegetables don't like sitting in wet soil, so if you have heavy soil, you will need to improve the texture. Organic matter should make a difference. However, you don't want all the nutrients to simply run off elsewhere. If you vegetable site isn't level, then you need to create run-off barriers. At the same time, you don't want water from less favorable sources such as the driveway to run into the vegetable garden.

Organic or Not

If you're like me, I was under the impression that organic gardening is more difficult and less successful than regular gardening with fertilizers and chemicals. I've found the opposite to be true. Today, garden centers are full of organic gardening products and more information is being written about organic gardening.

Organic gardening is less time consuming and easier than conventional gardening because the focus is on preventing problems. Soil that has a lot of organic matter is alive with organisms that benefit plants. When you keep your plants healthy with water, sun and nutrients then they will be able to ward off pests and diseases.

Tools

Every new activity you do around the house is going to require the proper tools. Vegetable gardening takes two stages: preparing the garden and caring for the plants. When creating a garden, you are going to be turning a lot of soil so you will at least need a shovel, fork, trowel and possibly a tiller. After you've planted your vegetables, you'll need a different set of tools. You'll at least need a garden hoe, hose and nozzle or irrigation system, stakes, twine, and pruners.

Fencing

The last thing to consider is fencing. This can be difficult, but you want to protect your vegetables. If you don't fence in your vegetables, then you will be fighting an endless battle against animals. In fact, you will likely want to consider a fence that goes above and below your garden. The fencing doesn't have to be fancy, but you at least want something protective to get you started.

PLANT IN THE FALL

While summer is often thought to be peak vegetable season, fall has the better qualities that make it more favorable for crops that like cooler temperatures and wetter conditions. During fall, the weather is milder, many insects and pests are getting ready to hibernate for the winter, the breeze keeps flying insects at bay, and the soil becomes the right combination of moist and well-draining.

While many vegetables grow and mature into the fall, most will need to be started before the nights turn cold. If you live in a climate where the frost comes early, then your garden will need to be started in mid-summer, sometime between late July through August. Even though daytime temperatures are high, evening temperatures are starting to fall and the length of daylight is decreasing. You want to choose varieties that have short days to maturity and get them in the ground on time.

PREPARATION

If you've been tending your garden in the summer with weeding, removing diseased or spent plants, and avoiding stepping on the soil, then you won't need to do much prep work at all. You'll only have to clear the space, maybe add some compost and then plant your new vegetables. However, most gardens are going to need a little attention before you start your next planting season. Use the following steps to prepare your garden.

Clean Up

Clear out as much as you can from your garden. Get rid of any weeds before they go to seed. Get rid of any plants that are done for the season and diseased. Clean up anything that has fallen off the plants since rotting fruits will attract pests. As you clean up, be sure to note where your plants were from the previous season in order to rotate your crops appropriately.

Move Mulch

You want to freshen your garden soil every year, and the easiest way to do this is to remove the layer of mulch. If it is in good condition, then you can re-use it for the fall. Most of it has likely already decomposed, so you'll probably need to add a little bit more.

For vegetable gardens, straw is an excellent mulch since it will easily scatter and move around the garden. It is also a good home for spiders who will help in controlling the pest population of the garden.

Another choice for fall mulch is shredded leaves. If you have a supply of fallen leaves, you can run them through a shredder or run them through a string weeder. Wet down the leaves, spread them around, and then place a light top dusting of compost to control them.

Soil Preparation

If your soil has been compacted during the summer, then you'll want to fluff it up with a garden fork. You don't need to do major tilling, just enough to allow new plant roots to move around and water to get through.

Fall is also a great time to test your soil. Many amendments will take time in order to have an impact on the soil. At the very least, you want to replenish the soil by adding some compost. You can either add it to the top, or you can work it in while loosening the soil. Before adding the compost, you need to have your planting layout done so you can add it where the plants will be growing and not along the walking paths.

If you are going to use manure, then you need to make sure it has thoroughly composted for at least six months. Fresh compost will burn the plant roots and cause a health risk to humans. I found the best option is to use slow-acting organic fertilizer while I'm loosening the soil. You can add amendments as needed if a soil test recommends it. Otherwise, a general purpose fertilizer will be fine. After you've adjusted the soil appropriately, then you need to rake it out to even out the surface and break up any clumps to create furrows that catch water.

KEEPING VEGETABLES GROWING

Vegetables don't require any more special care than other plants, but they are less forgiving of neglect. Vegetable plants take a lot of energy to bloom and produce fruit. Your job is to make sure you they have the necessary health and vigor needed to keep producing. Neglect can lead to lower yields and inferior vegetables because of an increase in pest problems.

Watering

Regular watering is as important for vegetables as sunlight. This means an inch or two of water per week, every week. If the weather is extremely hot, you'll need to have extra water. Without regular watering, vegetables won't fill out, and some will crack open if suddenly filled with water after not having it for a while.

You don't want to rely on rain. If you have the space, a drip irrigation system is a good option for a vegetable garden. Most of these systems are easy to install and are cheaper than some people think. You'll also save money on water since it will all be going directly to the roots with less evaporation. If you don't want a drip irrigation system, then try to place your garden near a water source so it will be easier to water every day.

Weeding

Vegetables don't like to compete for food or water. The biggest competition comes from weeds. With vegetables, you have the advantage of starting with an empty space each season. Before you plant, make sure you remove any existing weeds and keep everything weed free by cultivating a good layer of mulch.

Mulching

Mulching is the best thing for your vegetables. It reduces weeds, cools plant roots and helps conserve water. Sometimes the plants will provide living mulch if they grow thick enough. For a vegetable garden, the best mulch is seed-free straw. This provides a nice cover, is easy to push aside for planting and it can be turned into the soil at the end of the growing season. In addition, spiders will live in the straw to keep pests under control.

Feeding

Vegetables eat a lot. If you have enriched the soil, you won't have to do much supplemental feeding. You will want to work some organic matter into the soil each year before planting and side dress with organic matter once or twice during the growing season. Organic plant foods are slow releasing, so they will continue to feed your plants all season long. If you use a water-soluble fertilizer, then you want to make sure your garden is well-watered before applying.

WHAT TO PLANT

If you are planting a vegetable garden to increase your frugal living, then you want to plant vegetables that give a good return and are relatively easy and cheap to grow. Consider the best plants for your garden and determine what you have room to plant as well as what your family is most likely to eat a lot of during the year.

Peas

Peas are one of the first crops to plant in the spring and have a short season of 50-60 days, so they will be the first you harvest. Peas need well-drained soil and do well in raised beds and large planters. You need to provide them with a medium height trellis to climb. They should be sown thickly but can be sprouted indoors to help ensure success in damp conditions. Stagger the planting time by two weeks in order to extend the harvest. Peas will improve the soil by fixing nitrogen levels.

Lettuce

There are multiple varieties available. Large, head-forming lettuces such as Butterhead and Iceberg can be planted in single file rows to make mulching easier. Smaller, leafy varieties can be thickly planted for a self-mulching effect. You should ideally grow several varieties of each type. If temperatures are consistently too high, then a problem called bolting can occur. This is when the plant goes to seed, and the leaves stop growing. To prevent this, you want to plant lettuce in shaded areas, or plant them next to a shading crop such as tomatoes.

Broccoli

This vegetable is highly valued because of its nutritional value, long period of productivity and because broccoli costs a lot in the grocery store. Broccoli can be over-wintered, providing new shoots with small clusters of broccoli which are great through the winter. Sow broccoli directly from seed into the ground or in small starter pots. It is easier to protect them in starter pots from slugs and birds. In addition, when in pots, they can be moved indoors in inclement weather until they are strong enough to transplant. Broccoli crops should be grown in different beds and rotated each year.

Tomatoes

Tomatoes come in several varieties such as cherry, table, and paste. These plants need tall stakes, which should be set when you transplant the plants. Some people use wire cages. No matter what you choose, the plants need to be tied to the stakes as they grow. Tomatoes do best when the leaves are kept dry. Clear plastic sheeting can be used to shelter the plants. A layer of mulch will prevent rain splash from wetting the lower leaves and helps retain moisture in the upper soil. While transplants are growing in pots, till some green grass clippings into the soil where you are going to plant the tomatoes since this will warm the soil and give the young seedlings a boost when you transplant them.

Garlic

If you have a mild winter climate, then garlic can be planted in the fall before the frost. You can also plant garlic in early spring. They should be planted separate with the cloves base down at least two inches deep. To harvest, lift bulbs out when leaves die after plant blooms. Save a few heads for next season's crop.

Peppers

Peppers are typically started in small pots and transplanted when it is warm enough outside. Pick off small peppers that may form on transplants or the growth of the plant will be stunted. Pick green peppers as soon as they reach a size in order to stimulate new fruiting and increase the yield per plant. You can leave one or two plants unpicked if you want the peppers to sweeten and turn red or yellow. However, these plants will produce fewer peppers.

Onions and Leeks

These plants are slow to mature, about three to five months, and require moist soil with good drainage. Start with small bulbs if you want them to be mature in four to six weeks. Plant onions early in the season and sow thickly. Provide warmth early by covering the shoots with a row cover and tilling some green grass clippings into the soil before planting. When the onion tops turn yellow and wither, you can harvest them.

Swiss Chard

This vegetable is easy to grow with few pest problems and a long, productive season. You can grow it from transplants or directly sown into a garden bed. Avoid planting near spinach or beets.

Summer and Winter Squash

Zucchini and yellow squash are compact and easy to grow, which provide you with great summer vegetables. The winter varieties take more room to grow but are a highly valued winter vegetable. Squash should be planted individually in small hills, and for winter squash, there should be room for long vines and large leaves. If ground space in limited, you can grow squash vertically on a sturdy trellis. Each squash needs to be tied to the trellis by its stem in order to support the weight as it grows. Start the seeds indoors in small pots to protect them from squash bugs.

Beans

While beans come in many varieties, they can generally be classified into bush beans or pole beans. Bush beans grow about knee-high and can be planted in front of taller plants such as tomatoes. Pole beans grow tall and require support in the form of tall poles or a trellis. You should grow these to the back of the garden, so they don't shade other plants. Beans should be sown directly into the ground from seeds since they don't do well with transplanting. Stagger planting times in order to extend the harvest.

Potatoes

Potatoes are becoming a valued starchy food as the cost of bread increases. Potatoes are easy to grow, can take marginal soil and give a good yield for the space they require. New potatoes can be planted in mid-spring, just before the last frost. Winter varieties can be planted in early summer. Potatoes are planted directly into the ground in rows.

Blueberries

This is a highly nutritious perennial berry plant that grows to a waist-high shrub which should be planted along one of the side borders of your vegetable garden. The soil should be slightly acidic. Plant six to eight bushes for a reasonable harvest and plant at least two varieties to promote fertilization. Once the plant is three to four years old, prune out the older central shoots to stimulate new growth.

Vegetables are just the start to frugally growing and raising your own food. Another option that is fast becoming popular with city and country living people is raising backyard chickens. Let's discuss this simple task next.

RAISING LIVE CHICKENS

Chickens are an easy and inexpensive animal to raise compared to other pets. Fresh eggs are great-tasting and nutritious; plus it saves you money on the rising cost of eggs in the grocery store. Chickens provide your backyard garden with a chemical-free bug and weed control option. In addition, they provide a great source of fertilizer. With all these benefits, it is easy to see why many people are choosing to raise backyard chickens.

Before you decide to get chickens, you want to look into the local laws and ordinances in your area. If you live in a housing development, you should also check with the homeowner's association. Since chickens can be a little annoying in a small area, you should also check with your neighbors before bringing some chickens home. Consider promising them no roosters and offering free eggs on occasion so you can foster a good relationship with your neighbors.

The easiest way to get chickens is to purchase them through a local feed store. You can often get day old chicks from February to June. You can also hatch chickens from eggs, but this can be more difficult and time-consuming. You can also look online for people who are selling or giving away extra chickens they don't have room for.

For the first sixty days of a chick's life, you will need a chick brooder. The best flooring is pine shavings and corn cob. You don't want to use newspaper since it doesn't absorb well and can become slippery. For the first week, the temperature should be 90 to 100 degrees and then decrease at five degrees per week. Feed chick crumbles/starter and a chick waterer. While the chicks are still young, it is important to play with your chickens to get them used to be around people.

After the first sixty days, you can switch to general chicken care. Once feathered, you can move your chickens to a chicken coop. The coop should provide two to three square feet per chicken and four to five square feet per chicken in an outside run. Keep in mind any local predators to keep your flock safe. Again, pine shavings are best for flooring. You can also try a deep litter method for less maintenance. Most people choose to feed a formulated chicken layer feed/pellets. Some treat options include vegetables, bread, bugs and chicken scratch.

One good thing about growing and raising your own food choices is that you can preserve them for future use. You can enjoy fresh food while it is available, but preserve the rest for use later when your food supplies run low. This way you can save money on trips to the grocery store.

CANNING FOOD

Canning is an important and safe method of preserving extra food. The process involves placing foods in jars or similar containers and heating them to a temperature that destroys microorganisms that cause food to spoil. During the heating process, air is driven out of the jar and, as it cools, a vacuum seal is formed. This vacuum seal prevents air from getting back into the product and bringing in contaminating microorganisms.

There are two safe ways of canning food: the boiling water bath method and the pressure canner method.

Water Bath Method

Canned food has a shelf life of one to five years. Most fruits and acidic vegetables can be canned using the water bath method. This method involves placing food in sterilized canning jars, putting lids on them and then lowering them into water that comes to a boil. This method works best for the following foods:

- Jams and Jellies

- Fruit pieces such as peaches, apples, pears, pineapple, plums, etc.

- Salsas

- Tomatoes

- Chutneys

- Pickles

Pressure Canning Method

This is the method used for meats and most vegetables, anything low-acid. If you are putting high and low acid food together then you need to use this method. As with the water bath method, this process requires you to fill sterilized jars with food, cover with the appropriate lids and then place them in a pressure canner with boiling water in it. You then lock the pressure canner lid into place and vent it, allowing it to create steam for ten minutes. This method is best used for the following foods:

- Vegetables such as corn and green beans

- Soups and Stews

- Vegetable and Meat Stocks

- Meat

- Poultry

- Fish

PREPARING FOOD FOR CANNING

For specific times and techniques for the foods you want to can, it is best to get a current canning guide. Different foods require different processing for the canning method. The USDA has guidelines along with Ball or Kerr books that provide process times according to jar contents and size. Processing times have changed through the years because of new knowledge of food safety and because of a change in foods. For example, tomatoes today have far less acid than they used to have.

Wash your hands thoroughly at the start of the process and keep them clean throughout the process. The goal is to reduce the amount of bacteria that can contaminate the canned food. If you sneeze, visit the bathroom or handle non-food items during the process, then you should wash your hands again.

Most food needs to be cut up in order to fit more easily into jars. Peel and cut up fruits or vegetables. Remove pits, stems, cores and any other parts you don't eat. Jam should be cooked. Pickles need to be cooked and/or soaked. Relish, applesauce, apple butter and other foods need to be prepared according to their recipes.

If a recipe calls for it, then you need to make a canning liquid. Most fruits and vegetables are canned in either syrup or brine. Syrup uses a mixture of water or juice and sugar while brine uses a mixture of water and salt. A canning book will provide you the proper mixture for the specific liquid needed.

STERILIZING THE JARS

Mason jars can be sterilized by boiling them in water for ten minutes. You need to sterilize the jars because if there are any bacteria in them when you put food in them and seal them; your canned food will go bad. If you are at a high altitude, then you need to add an additional minute for each 1,000 feet above sea level. After boiling, place them upside-down on a clean towel and drape another towel over them until you are ready to use them. They can also be sterilized in the dishwasher.

Boil about an inch of water in the bottom of a medium saucepan. Remove the pan from the heat. Place the jar seals into the water and push them down so they sink. Avoid stacking them on top of each other so they heat evenly. Allow them to soften for a minute or two. If you time it right, you can start this step while you fill jars and wipe rims.

CANNING FOOD

Filling the jars is also known as packing the jars. Foods are either "hot-packed" or "cold-packed" depending on whether they are cooked and packed into jars hot or simply cut up and packed into jars cold. This difference will impact the cooking time for food, so again you need to follow the recipe carefully.

You should leave a little bit of space at the top, known as "head space." This can vary from an eighth of an inch to an inch depending on the food. Check the instructions in the recipe carefully.

Some common preservatives used in home canning include sugar, salt, and acids like lemon juice and ascorbic acid or Vitamin C sold in powder form. This preservative should be added before the liquid so that it mixed in properly.

Pour the syrup or preserving liquid into the jar and leave about a half inch of space at the top of the jar.

When you pour liquid over loose pieces, you'll leave air bubbles behind. Remove these bubbles by running a long, plastic knife down the side and jiggling or gently pressing the food.

Wipe the rims and threads of the jars with a clean, damp cloth in order to remove residue or drips. Pay special attention to clean the top surface where the seal will sit.

Place a softened seal on each jar. A magnetic lid wand helps get them safely out of the boiling water. To release a seal, set it on a jar and tilt the wand. Alternatively, you can use a small pair of tongs. Just don't touch the lids with your hands.

Lastly, screw a clean ring down over the seal and tighten it. However, don't tighten so much that you press all the seal material off the rim.

USING A CANNER

If your recipe calls for it, you will need to use a water bath canner. This works for many cooked foods and acid fruits. Lower the jars into a rack in a water bath canner or large stock pot. Add enough water to cover them by one to two inches. Add hot water if the jars are hot packed and cold water if the jars are cold packed. Avoid sudden and drastic temperature changes and avoid stacking the jars.

If you use a large stock pot, place a rack or other spacer on the bottom of the pot, so the jars don't rest directly on the bottom. Cover the canner and bring the water to a gentle boil. Boil for the specified time according to the recipe.

Some recipes call for the use of a pressure canner. This is necessary for meats and most vegetables because they don't have enough acid in them. Pressure canning can also reduce the processing time for foods such as peaches and tomatoes, compared to the water bath canning method.

Arrange the jars in the pressure canner carefully. You may be able to stack smaller jars as long as they are offset.

Check the gasket before you start pressure canning each year. The gaskets tend to dry out over time. The gasket should be able to form a seal. You can revive a dry gasket by soaking it in just-boiled water. If the gasket is too old or cracked, it should be replaced. Ideally, a gasket is replaced every year or two.

Place the lid on the pressure canner and twist it firmly closed. The handle position will often tell you if it is closed. Remove the rocker from the lid of the canner.

Bring the pressure canner to a boil. Watch the steam coming out of the opening where the rocker will go. It often also has an indicator pin in the center. This pin will pop up as steam builds within the canner.

Allow the steam to vent for a period of time. Let it vent for at least seven minutes with a strong, even stream. Or for the specified time in your recipe.

Place the rocker on the vent and start timing the specific process time. The needle on the pressure gauge should start to rise.

Adjust the temperature on the stove so that the pressure in the canner is the same as that specified in the recipe. You'll often have to make multiple small adjustments to get the pressure right. It takes a few moments to see the effects of each adjustment.

Stay with the pressure canner for the entire cooking process, adjusting the temperature as needed. Drafts and other variations can cause the temperature to shift. Don't assume you've reached a balance point since the pressure can be disrupted fairly quickly. If the pressure is too low, it can fail to cook sufficiently hot, and one that is too high can run the risk of breakage.

Process the jars for the full time stated in the recipe and then turn off the heat. Leave the rocker on until the indicator pin drops. Once the pin drops, remove the rocker and allow the canner to vent for a few minutes.

Open the lid slowly and keep it between yourself and the jars for a few moments. While it doesn't happen often, the jars occasionally break when the pressure is released.

HANDLING PROCESSED JARS

Remove the jars from the canner with jar tongs. Place the jars on a clean towel to cool. Allow the full jars to cool for 24 hours in a place free from drafts. Don't touch the lids and let them seal on their own.

After several hours have passed, make sure the jars are sealed. The dome lid should be pulled down very tightly. If you can press the center of the lid down, then it did not seal properly. If any of the jars aren't sealed, you can place a fresh lid on them and process them again or refrigerate those jars and use the contents soon.

Wash the jars in room temperature, soapy water to remove any residue on the outside. At this point, you can remove the rings since the seals should be holding themselves. Allow the rings and jars to dry thoroughly before replacing the rings in order to prevent rust.

Label your canned goods with the year. You may also want to label them with contents. It is best to place the label on the seals rather than the glass if you are going to reuse the jars. Store sealed jars on the shelf and avoid excessive exposure to heat or light. Once you open the jars, keep them refrigerated.

Canning is just one method of preserving food for later use. There are a variety of other options and what you choose should depend on how soon you will use the food, space and location you have for preserving and the type of food you are preserving. Let's look at some of the other options.

HOW TO PRESERVE AND STORE EXTRA FOOD

There are many ways to preserve extra food. Aside from canning that we just learned about, most people are only familiar with refrigeration and freezing. In order to take advantage of preserving food and living frugally, I took the time to learn about all the methods of preservation there are today. Let's take a look at what I learned, and I'll let you determine which methods are best for you.

REFRIGERATING AND FREEZING FOOD

Keeping food cold prevents a lot of bacteria from forming. Most people are familiar with these methods. Refrigeration is good for food that you will be eating relatively soon; about three to five days for meats, fruits and vegetables and a week or so for dairy products. Condiments can be good for months. If you aren't sure about something, then err on the side of caution and don't eat it.

Food should be placed in airtight containers. This is especially true for leftovers and other foods that haven't been packaged at a store. This allows the food to maintain its freshness in the refrigerator. Meat from the store should be left in its packages until you use them. Don't store fruits with vegetables. For vegetables, remove any ties or rubber bands before refrigerating and pack loosely in the refrigerator.

The refrigerator itself should be organized. The top of the fridge has the most consistent temperature and is best for leftovers and other items that don't need to be cooked. The door is the warmest location and is best for drinks and condiments. Fruits and vegetables should be kept in the crisper drawers at the bottom where you can keep them separated and moist. The bottom shelves are the coldest and should be used for raw meat and eggs.

For longer term storage you should freeze foods. Never pack your freezer too tight with food since the cold air needs to circulate between all of the items in order to have the freezer work properly. Frozen foods can last from six months to a year.

Foods need to be packaged properly before freezing. The best option is vacuum packing. If you don't have a vacuum sealer, at least try to get as much air out of the bags as possible before sealing. Label everything with contents and date with freezer-friendly masking tape. You should never freeze glass containers. Don't fill containers to the top with leftovers before freezing since they will expand. Don't put hot food into the freezer. Don't thaw and re-freeze food since it will degrade quickly.

DRYING FOODS

Dehydrating

When you dehydrate your food, you take all the liquids out of it. Once the food is fully dehydrated, it is very difficult for bacteria to form. This allows the food to last for weeks or months without refrigeration. The food maintains the same fiber and calories content, except for a loss of Vitamin C in some foods because of solubility. A food dehydrator allows you to preserve fruits, vegetables, and meats.

If you don't want to buy a dehydrator, then you can get the same effect with a low-temperature oven. With the oven on the lowest possible setting, you can place your food on a non-stick pan and use a small fan to keep the air circulating and prevent any moisture from building up on the food. This process will take all of the liquid out of the foods and preserve them in a chewier form.

Smoking

Smoking meats have been a method of preservation for thousands of years. The kind of wood for the fire and the spices you put on the meat can give you an array of wonderful flavors. There are two kinds of smoking: hot and cold.

With the hot method, you are cooking the meat at a low temperature for a long time.

With the cold method, you aren't meant to cook the meat at all; rather you are sealing the meat enough so bacteria can't grow. This method works well if you are going to cook the meat at some point in the future.

Curing

Like smoking, curing is a process that has been used for thousands of years. This process uses salt to remove the water from meat and dehydrate it. There are two ways that you can cure meat.

Dry curing involves rubbing the meat with salt and sodium nitrite along with other spices of your choosing. The meat is then hung to dry.

Wet curing or brining also uses salt, but in a liquid solution. Meat is placed into a brine mixture of water, salt, sodium nitrite and other spices.

Pickling

Pickling can apply to multiple processes that usually involve fermentation and canning, though it might only be one or the other. The usual pickling process is for cucumber pickles that involve canning in a vinegar brine. The process can be used for a number of other fruits and vegetables including the following:

- Okra

- Peppers

- Ginger

- Green Beans

- Brussels Sprouts

- Cauliflower

- Eggplant

- Watermelon Rinds

- Lemons

- Pineapple

Fermenting

You can ferment cucumbers or cabbage to make pickles and sauerkraut. This process typically takes three weeks. The vegetables are salted and put into a pickling crock. The water comes out of the vegetable as it ferments and creates a new flavor.

PACKAGING METHODS

Bulk foods can also be stored in different types of containers. You should make sure you are using food grade containers that exclude light, oxygen and moisture. This can help extend the shelf life of food. Let's look at the various packaging methods you have to choose from.

5 or 6 Gallon Plastic Buckets or Pails

These buckets have tight fitting lids with rubber gaskets. These are great for large amounts of grains, beans, legumes, sugar, flour, etc. You can purchase an inner liner made from metalized foil. This liner prevents lights from harming the food and causing it to deteriorate. The liner also acts as a moisture barrier and to keep rodents out of the food. After lining the bucket, fumigate with either the dry ice method or nitrogen flushing or oxygen absorber packets. Then you want to get out as much air as possible. Lay the bag flat and use an iron to heat seal the end of the bag so you can use it again and again. Pierce a hole in the corner of the bag, hold the bag below the seal, so you don't suck up the contents of the bag. Suck all the air out with a hose or a smaller attachment to the vacuum that can be inserted into the end. Once the air is sucked out and the bag looks vacuum packed, hold the end and seal it with an iron. Don't let air back into the bag.

#10 Size Double Enamel Cans

These cans hold about one gallon and are ideal for smaller quantities of food. You can purchase plastic lids to put on the cans once they are opened. These types of containers are used by most food storage companies. They are nitrogen packed with an oxygen absorber packet sealed inside the can. The packets absorb free oxygen from the air around them and chemically bind it. This removes the oxygen from inside the can, which prevents insects from hatching or even living. Since the atmosphere inside the can is mostly nitrogen, this is ideal for long term food storage.

WHERE TO STORE FOOD

Before you store your food, you need to find the right place that has the appropriate conditions, relative convenience, and sufficient space. If you have room, you should find a room in your home to dedicate for food storage.

Food should be stored in a cool, dry place away from sunlight. Find the coolest place in your home. This is often the basement if you have one, but any place away from a furnace or other heat source will work. Some good locations are root cellars, insulated and heated garages, spare bedrooms, unfinished rooms, crawl spaces, closets, under stairways or under beds. North walls are always cooler because they are away from sun exposure.

The room you choose should be dry at all times. If your clothes dryer happens to be in the same room, it should be properly ventilated in order to prevent moisture from gathering on the food.

It is also important that you locate your food storage area near to the kitchen. This makes it easier to rotate food storage. Let's look at a few of the better areas to store your food.

Basement

If you have a basement, the temperature is often cooler and ideal for storing food. Keep your food away from dryer vents or furnaces, which give off moisture that can rust cans.

Under Stairways

The space under a stairway is often wasted since the sloped ceiling makes it inappropriate for a variety of uses. You can build in shelves that hold food such as canned goods, large buckets, and even some camping equipment.

Closets

You can easily turn a closet into a pantry. You will often be surprised at how much a closet will hold when you properly install shelving. Be sure to measure all boxes and cans so you can properly install shelving.

Garage

If your garage temperature fluctuates between freezing and hot, then you probably don't want to use your garage for food storage.

If food can stay at a relatively consistent temperature, then it will retain its nutrient value about fifty percent longer. However, a garage can be an excellent option for short-term emergency equipment storage.

Attic

You shouldn't store food in your attic if it heats up in the summer. The food will spoil quickly in hot temperatures. If you have a vented and insulated attic that stays at a fairly consistent temperature, then it can work for storing food. Just remember that the further you store food away from the kitchen the harder it will be to get when you need something.

ROTATION AND DETERIORATION OF FOOD STORAGE

In addition to the limited shelf life, food is susceptible to deterioration and spoilage from a variety of natural causes. Aside from avoiding the elements that result in food deterioration, you can take some additional steps to help prevent food spoilage. You can use any of the following methods depending on the food you are storing, the containers used and what storage problems you are most likely to face.

Oxygen Absorber Packets

This newer option is also becoming one of the best methods for preserving food. This is the safest way to remove oxygen from stored food containers. Here is a picture of them, you can find them in most stores like Wal-Mart, and other grocery and food supply stores, but we found EBay being the cheapest of them all so far.

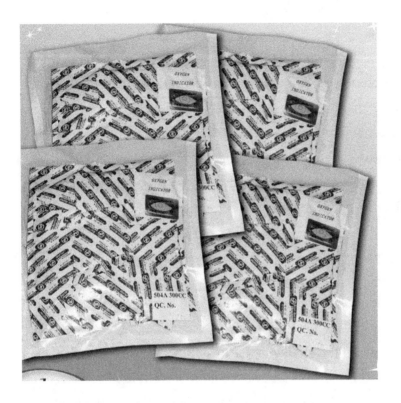

Bay Leaves

When you put bay leaves into your grain and spread them throughout the container, you can discourage bug infestation. Since bugs don't like the smell of bay leaves, they are deterred from getting into food. Two bay leaves per gallon is enough to do the job.

Let's finish up our segment on food by discussing how to start fishing. This is an excellent way to get a good source of protein for cheap.

FISHING: HOW TO START AND BE SUCCESSFUL

Thankfully, I had a grandfather and father who were into fishing, so I learned quite a bit from them. However, I realize there are individuals out there who may not have a clue about where to start when it comes to fishing. Fishing certainly requires some skill, but also a lot of patience. If you want your frugal budget to spread, then learning to fish is certainly a way to gain a good source of cheap protein. So let me help you get started with fishing.

GEARING UP

If you go to the fishing isle of your local sporting store you are going to be surprised at the number of equipment options. While you can certainly add more equipment as you get more experienced and find out what works for you; I find it better to start with just the simple basics until you know a little more about fishing.

Of course, the first thing you are going to need is a rod and reel. For beginners, it is best to choose a simple, versatile and foolproof option. There are three options that fit these goals:

1. A bait casting outfit

2. A spin-casting set

3. An open-faced spinning reel and matching rod

My best suggestion is to get a medium-sized, open-faced spinning reel and a medium action, six to seven-foot fiberglass spinning rod. With this setup and a few lures, hooks and sinkers, you will be ready to go freshwater fishing in most types of water and maybe even a few smaller saltwater species.

Tackle

Tackle includes all the hooks, sinkers, bobbers and artificial lures that you'll be attaching to the end of your line. At this time just focus on getting the basics until you start to get a handle on what works best for you and attracts the most success in the area you fish.

Bait

While artificial lures will catch fish, they aren't as good as using live bait. For freshwater fishing, the best bait option is earthworms. Other good options include minnows, crayfish, frogs, crickets, grasshoppers, salamanders and pretty much anything else fish routinely eat.

GETTING IN THE WATER

The tactics you will use to fish depends largely on the water you're fishing in and the species of fish you want to catch. I'll discuss some of the basics in the most common areas you'll fish, just determine which matches the setting you'll be fishing in and take the time to try things a little different until you find what works for you.

Pond Fishing

This is the most laid back setting for fishing. Here you'll typically be fishing for bream, catfish, bass, carp or suckers. If the pond is deep enough to be cold and oxygen-rich year round, then you may also be able to catch trout. Just make sure the pond you are fishing in isn't owned by anyone and if it is, seek permission before fishing.

The most common way to fish a pond or any other small, still body of water is with a bobber, hook, worms and a small split shot sinker. Start with a six or eight sized hook, thread the worm on the hook, clamp the split shot a few inches to a foot above the bait, and fix the bobber to the line at a point where the worm will float just above the bottom of the pond.

Once you cast, keep the line relatively tight, but not enough to drag the bobber. Once you see the bobber drag along the surface of the water or if it gets pulled under then give the rod a short, sharp jerk to set the hook and reel in your fish.

Lakes, Slow Rivers, and Ocean Shores

The tactics for a pond will also work in larger bodies of water as long as the artificial lures are suited to the fish available or you are using the appropriate bait. However, there is another type of still-fishing that is commonly used on bigger water that can be very effective. Known as bottom fishing, it requires a heavier sinker and one or more hooks to hold the bait on or just above the bottom after a long cast. Bottom fishing typically works best with live bait and a terminal rig. In general, it is best to have a tight line so you can see the rod tip move to signal a feeding fish.

Streams and Fast Rivers

There are plenty of fish in streams and fast rivers, but this kind of fishing is usually dedicated to fly-fishing. This is a wonderful option, but beyond the scope of basic beginning fishing. There are a number of articles and books that can get you started on fly-fishing if you become experienced enough with general fishing and want to move on to something more advanced like fly-fishing.

Again this is just the basics to get you started. Once you are comfortable with the basics of fishing you can choose to expand into more complicated areas. For now, let's move on.

5 WAYS TO SAVE MONEY ON ENTERTAINMENT

Just because you're living frugally don't mean you have to avoid entertainment. Even with a strict budget, there are ways you can save on entertainment and still have some fun on occasion. Consider the following five ways you can save money on entertainment.

1. Plan Your Visit

Theaters, museums, galleries, zoos and parks all have special discount days. This can be standing room only, pay-what-you-can and even free admission. Some amusement and water parks also offer twilight discounts where you can save 30-50% off just by coming closer to closing time. Be sure to check out the locations website to see what discount days they offer and then plan your visit accordingly.

2. Theater Discounts

Most theaters have a discount day. There are certain days where movie tickets are discounted all day. This would be the best time to go to see a movie without having to wait for it to come out on DVD.

3. Go Used

While most people have gone digital these days, if you still want a DVD or CD for cheap then you can consider buying used. There are a number of websites online or thrift stores in your area where you can buy used DVDs and CDs for cheap. In addition, there are more websites that allow you to swap entertainment such as TitleTrader.com and SwapTree.com. These services are free, but you do have to pay for shipping.

4. Explore Outdoors

The great outdoors provides you with plenty of free and cheap entertainment. State and national parks are an inexpensive way to get out and enjoy nature. When you buy a year's pass, you can really save money on your entertainment.

5. Stay Indoors

Of course, when the weather isn't favorable you can't just go to your local park and take a hike. For these days consider staying inside and doing something fun like a board game or a puzzle. It will allow time to pass quickly and give you a chance to bond as a family. Alternatively, you can go on the computer and find a video game to play. There are websites such as NickJr.com which provide plenty of free video games that are fun and educational for children of all ages.

Although if you are like me, you may just want to stay indoors and watch movies. The rising cost of cable is something that really hits your budget. So let us take a look at six ways you can reduce your cable bill and still enjoy some in home entertainment.

In just a few years the average cable bill went from $80 to over $150 per month. That is a lot of money for television. Even if you can get a discounted package, these often only last for a year before going up in price. If you want to reduce your cable bill, then consider the following six tips.

1. Drop Premium Channels

If you don't want to entirely get rid of cable, then you should at least consider getting rid of premium channels. If you find yourself only watching one or two shows a week, then consider a lower monthly plan to save money. However, if you really are only watching one or two shows a week, there are a lot of cheaper options to consider below.

2. Negotiate with Your Provider

Ask for them to trim your monthly bill and if they don't work with you, tell them you'll switch to another provider. Be polite, but firm in your negotiation, and you'll be surprised at how much they are willing to work with you to decrease your monthly bill.

3. HDTV Antenna

If you have an over-the-air antenna, then you might be able to get high-definition broadcasts from local TV stations for free.

4. Streaming Media

You can get a device such as Apple TV, Roku, and Google Chromecast in order to get streaming video services to your TV.

You can also access these subscription-based services through Net-connected smart TVs, Blu-ray players, and video game consoles. This option can also save you a lot of money on the cost of cable since you get the same amount of programming for a fraction of the cost.

5. Go Online

A lot of the popular TV shows can be found online at official network TV websites. Sometimes you can even get episodes the day after their air. Even with a service such as Hulu.com; paying for a single season of a show you watch may be cheaper than paying for a cable subscription.

6. Go Mobile

There are several apps that can offer streaming videos to your smartphones and tablets. This way you can watch your TV shows no matter where you go.

Any of these six strategies can save you money on your cable bill while still allowing you to watch your favorite TV shows. Just because you're living frugally, doesn't mean you need to completely remove all fun from your life. Let's now discuss some apps you can get that will help you save little bits of money throughout the day.

7 APPS AND WEBSITES TO HELP YOU SAVE MONEY

Nearly everyone carries a smartphone with them these days, and there are several apps that can help you save on everything from you gas bill to everyday budgeting. The smartphone is a wonderful tool. Consider these apps and websites to help you save even more money.

1. **Save Money on Clothes**

ThredUp is the largest online consignment and thrift store. Most of the clothing on this website is for women and children, but there is a selection for men. In addition to purchasing clothing; you also have the option of selling your used clothes on consignment. Spend over $50, and you get free shipping. A great website if you want to save some money on buying clothes.

2. **Save Money on Gas**

GasBuddy is the best app to help you find the lowest prices for gas in the United States and Canada. Just enter your location, and it will give you the cheapest gas in your area. This way you can always be sure you are getting the lowest price possible to fill up your tank.

3. **Find Coupons Easily**

Coupons.com is a great website where you will find a number of printable and online coupons. You can pretty much get a coupon for anything on this website. Rather than waiting to search through newspapers for coupons, this website allows you to access the coupons you need when you need them. The website also has a mobile app called GroceryIQ that can help you get mobile coupons.

4. Save Money on Food

Paprika is a wonderful all around website. It allows you to look up recipes from a number of websites and then also helps you with meal planning and generating a grocery list. This is great for the frugal individual who wants to plan meals in advance to save money. Then when you go to the grocery store, you can stick to your list without buying anything extra you don't need.

5. Save Money on Everything

RedLaser is a price-comparison app you can load onto your smartphone. Then when you're shopping, you just scan the UPC barcode with the app, and it will pull up competing prices for the same item. You can block retailers that you don't want to see so you can reduce the list just to retailers you prefer to shop at while out on the town. This way, before making a purchase, you can be sure you are getting the best price possible.

6. Develop and Maintain a Budget

You Need a Budget is a wonderful tool that will help you track your spending and help with your budgeting. This tool makes it easy to track your expenses and look at the data in a way that helps you to find the holes in your budget. The nice part is you don't have to enter any account information, so all your data stays private. There is a mobile and desktop version; both of which can be synced together.

7. Simplify Your Accounts

BillGuard is a wonderful app that lets you combine all your financial information into a single viewpoint, showing your total financial progress. This app also allows you to see offers from various financial companies so you can get the best rates. The app also works well to protect you financially since it requires you to approve each transaction individually, so no errors or fraud occurs.

HOW TO TRAVEL FOR CHEAP

Everyone's heard the old saying "the best things in life are always free". This can be true when you are living a frugal life. Even if things aren't actually free, you will be amazed at the number of things you can do for cheap. Let's take a moment just to consider how you can travel for cheap. Everyone needs a vacation once in a while, but no one wants to save up for years just to have a short vacation. I'm going to show you how you can travel for cheap.

HOW TO BOOK CHEAP FLIGHTS

The cost of airline tickets varies considerably day to day and even among airlines. Sometimes prices can vary so greatly that no two seats on the same flight cost the same unless purchased together. There are a few tips you can use to help you get the best and cheapest price possible on your airline tickets.

SEARCHING APPROPRIATELY

Compare Using Accurate and Fair Search Engines

In order to find the cheapest flights, you are going to have to take the time to do a rigorous search. This search will require multiple search engine and airlines. However, most airfare search engines are actually owned or operated by the major airlines so they don't give you an unbiased search. Rather than sticking with a search engine you see advertised on television; you should use a search engine that looks for the cheapest fares among both large and small airlines.

Search Nearby Airports

This is a simple and effective way to find a cheap flight. Sometimes a flight from the local airport to your destination can be expensive while a flight from a nearby airport can be far cheaper. So consider if driving or taking a bus to a nearby airport is a cheaper way to get to your destination.

Visit Airline Websites

While airfare search engines simplify the process, sometimes the best deals are reserved for people who visit the actual airline's website. Search for a list of the carriers in your area and then do a search on their sites and see what deals they offer. Often if there is going to be a coupon, discount or sale they will only be offered through the specific carrier's website and only for a few days at a time.

Sign up for Travel Alerts

While getting spammed with emails doesn't seem like the best option, getting travel alerts to your email can be a great way to get an amazing price that you wouldn't otherwise have access to through other means. If your favorite airline or airfare search engines offers travel alerts to your phone or email, then sign up as soon as possible. It will only take seconds to delete unwanted messages when in comparison you can get a single email that saves you hundreds of dollars on your airfare.

Social Media Sites

Consider "Liking" an airline page on Facebook or following them on Twitter, when you do so you can receive special offers. Airlines will reward regular customers and encourage them to continue using their services. As a result, they will often advertise special low rates and discounts through their social media sites only. Follow as many airlines as you can in order to increase your chances of getting a great deal.

Searching at the Right Time

There is a right time and wrong time to search for cheaper airline tickets. Several studies have found that it is best to search for airline tickets around three in the afternoon on Tuesday. This is when most airlines release their discounted flight options, and at the same time, they are looking to fill up last-minute flights for the coming weekend.

However, searching on the right day and time isn't all there is to it. You also need to search for a specific number of days from your flight in order to get the lowest price. At the earliest, you should begin your search three months before your flight and at the latest 18 days before your flight. Studies have found that the best deals are posted for flights about six weeks before takeoff, so aim for about a month and a half before you trip in order to get the best deals on airline tickets.

Use Multiple Airlines

While looking for a flight on a single airline may seem like the easiest option, you will get better results when you fly on multiple airlines. Consider using one airline to get to your destination and then another to return. Or consider changing to another airline during a layover. When you break up your trip and split it between carriers, you will likely save enough money to make it worth the time and hassle.

Book Together

Depending on where you're traveling, you are going to need a flight, hotel and car at the very least. Rather than trying to organize them all separately, you can save both time and money by booking them together. While it may seem like you are spending more money in the short term, you are actually saving money by going with a package deal.

Use Your Miles

For frequent fliers, it is always a good idea to check your miles. You may find you have enough to get at least one free flight. Or perhaps you will get enough points on your way to your destination in order to get a free return flight.

Check for Discounts

There are quite a few discounts you can take advantage of when getting airline tickets. Students, military and senior deals are some of the most common. Check the airline's website and see what discounts they offer to see whether or not you qualify for one of them.

The Right Day to Fly

Leaving for your trip Friday after work or on Sunday after a relaxing weekend may seem like the best options, but these are actually the worst times to fly. Since there is a higher traffic of fliers on these days, the prices are increased. If possible, you should adjust your plans to fly on a Wednesday, Tuesday or Saturday for the best deals. Mid-week departures are the slowest, so carriers offer lower deals in order to fill seats.

In addition, the earlier you leave on a flight is going to be the cheapest. Red eye flights are the cheapest, followed by early morning flights. Typically the later in the day you leave the more expensive your airline ticket will be.

Stay with Economy

Obviously, the best way to save money is to sacrifice some creature comforts. You can save hundreds of dollars by choosing to fly in 4th or 5th class as opposed to 1st or 2nd. While you may not have leg room or dinner menu, you will be saving a lot of money.

Be Flexible on Dates

A lot of airlines also have minimum and maximum requirements for the number of days you spend in a location in order to get the best deal. In order to get the cheapest flights, you should stay a minimum of two nights and a maximum of 30. Ideally, stay at your destination over the weekend since flights that bookend a Saturday night are cheaper than those that lack a Saturday stay.

Choose Indirect Flights

Layovers are difficult, especially if you have to deal with several of them. However, when you fly indirectly to your location you are reducing the total cost of your flight. Direct flights are popular and in demand, so they are more expensive. Consider at least one layover and prepare for more in order to save money.

Choose Smaller Airlines

It is often considered easier and safer to stick with the major airlines, but when you consider using a smaller carrier you can save money. Often small, area-specific airlines may provide lower prices as an incentive to get people to fly with them over the larger carriers. Search for budget carriers in your area and destination to see what prices they offer before making your final decision.

Consider Alternative Routes

This is a little different than flying the indirect route with layovers. If you don't need to get to your destination by a specific time, then consider alternative routes. Book two separate flights if it is cheaper. While breaking up your travel will increase the amount of time you need to spend getting to your destination; it can be one of the best ways to save money.

These are just a few ways to save money on the airline flight to your destination. However, you also need to save money once you reach your destination. Consider the following tips to help with this aspect of your travel.

50 MUST TRY MONEY SAVING TRAVEL TIPS THAT WORK

1. Stay at a B&B instead of a hotel. In most countries, a B&B offers a warm and cultural place to stay for half the price of a standard hotel.

2. Avoid going to a restaurant clearly targeted to tourists. These are the restaurants that advertise they speak English or have multilingual menus. Often a local restaurant is not only going to be cheaper, but it's going to give you better food as well. To save extra money, always order the daily specials.

3. Consider flying into one country and out of another. This way you avoid the cost of returning to your starting point, and you can have an enjoyable adventure. For example, start in England and work your way into Turkey before heading home.

4. Traveling off season in October through April in Europe is an excellent option. During this time you will get cheaper airfare, budget rooms, and fewer tourists.

5. You will get the best value at family run businesses. Mom and pop shops care more about their reputation and their customers, rather than making a profit.

6. When you first arrive, stock up on drinks and munchies for your hotel room. Then pack an enjoyable picnic meal to save money while having an enjoyable day exploring around town.

7. When you order what's in season, you'll get more food for less money.

8. Save money with a guidebook. They can cost you about $20 but will get you upwards of $3,000 in savings. You can easily make a guidebook pay for itself in the first day.

9. ATMs are the cheaper and faster way to get your cash compared to traveler checks. While they do charge transaction fees, you can minimize these by making fewer and larger withdrawals.

10. Dial direct to keep in contact for cheap. International phone cards with PIN numbers can be bought at newsstands pretty much anywhere. You can make a call for as little as ten cents a minute.

11. Rent a car only if you are going to need to drive long distances. Otherwise, use public transportation or walk to see the city.

12. Shop in cheaper countries. If you are going to buy souvenirs do it where your dollar will stretch more. In addition, you're likely to get more interesting gifts.

13. If you know any family or friends in the area, look them up and see if you can stay with them.

14. Adapt to local tastes. Go with the local specialties in order to get the best service and price.

15. Consider consolidator tickets for overseas flights. You may have to put up with a few minor drawbacks such as

no changes and no frequent flier miles, but you will save a lot of money.

16. Base your choice of flight, car rental and hotel on the best value and not how many extra mile points you will get.

17. Consider the pass options for local transportation. Sometimes getting a rail pass or bus pass can get you around town cheaper than renting a car or using a cab.

18. Always go second-class. Nearly all transportation options offer a first and second class option. Often the difference in comfort is minimal, but the cost savings can be drastic.

19. Traveling by bus is often slower, but can be your cheapest option depending on where you are traveling.

20. If you're traveling in a group, then save money by sharing a car. This is the time when renting a car can be cheaper than choosing public transportation.

21. Choose your parking carefully. Thieves target tourist cars. It can be a good investment to spend a little more to park in a garage with an attendant.

22. If you choose public transportation, see if they offer any additional discounts. For example, in some European countries, you get a discount on bike rentals at the train station for ticket holders. This can be a great way to get around and see the sights without spending a lot of money.

23. If possible, you should pay with cash and not credit cards. While credit cards offer a good exchange rate, many smaller mom and pop places that have better deals will only accept cash.

24. If you need to change cash, avoid going to exchange bureaus that don't advertise buying and selling rates. When you see both rates, you can determine the profit margin, which should always be within five percent. If a place only shows the selling rate, then they are hiding something.

25. You don't want to waste your money by losing it. Be wary of pickpockets, beggars and commotions in crowds. Consider wearing a money belt to protect your cash.

26. Always ask for a discount. Often students, families, seniors and military get discounts.

27. Be sure you understand all expenses and fees involved in any transaction. Always ask for an itemized bill and assume you'll be short-changed. Ask how much something is and do your own math without letting the cashier rush you. When you shop savvy, you will save a lot of money.

28. If possible, you should travel with a partner. Not only does this give you someone to share the adventure with, but you both will save money. You can split the cost of hotels, taxis, guidebooks, and food.

29. Buy maps when you get to your destination and not before. Maps are often half the price at your destination and have a wider selection.

30. Rather than wasting money mailing postcards, do all your communications online. You can often get free internet access at libraries, hotels, and hostels.

31. Save money on your hotel costs by considering a hostel instead. Get a hostel card, and you can save on your cost of a hotel room. Most hostels also come with a kitchen that allows you to cook your groceries to even save money on food as well.

32. For cheap souvenirs and trinkets, you should always take advantage of department stores. In addition, you can find cheap cafeterias and restaurants at department stores as well.

33. Flea markets can be a rip-off for tourists, but they can also be a place to get great deals. Prices are soft, so take the time to haggle, and you're sure to get a great deal.

34. Once you get to your destination, consider using a budget airline to connect cities. While larger airlines can get you from city to city faster; you are likely to get better deals going with smaller, budget airlines.

35. No matter where you go, you can save money by enjoying the great outdoors. Consider camping or just taking a day hike.

36. Be aware of your hotel's cancellation policy and keep track of your reservations. No shows are often charged for a single night. If you can't make it for any reason, then cancel long in advance. Reconfirm all hotel reservations two days in advance. Even the best of hotels can mess up bookings. If you arrive to find no room, then this can be a costly issue to deal with.

37. Don't use a travel agent or tourist office to find a hotel room. They will often charge a fee and often only find you the highest-priced rooms with no discount. Use your guidebook, shop around on your own or go directly in order to get the best value for your accommodations.

38. Look for rooms at the last minute and check out business hotels for off-peak deals. If you arrive without reservations when business traffic is slow, you can often get a great deal. This is often during the summer months and weekends.

39. Consider budget chain hotels. This can often be great savings for traveling families.

40. Be smart about your hotel choices. A three-star hotel is a bad value for those traveling on a budget if they're satisfied with one-star service. Before accepting a room, ask to see it.

41. If the business is slow for a hotel then just come out and ask for a discount on your room. Other times you can get a discount if you offer to pay in cash or stay at least three nights.

42. The more people you can fit in a hotel room, the cheaper it gets per person. If you can deal with more people in a room, then just use one room rather than two.

43. Avoid the breakfast at a hotel. While this can be convenient, they often aren't a good value. If breakfast is optional, you can save money by going to the local corner cafe for breakfast.

44. Throughout most countries, it can be cheaper to get drinks at the bar rather than the table. Going to the bar for a quick drink can often be half the cost of getting seated at a table to enjoy a slow drink.

45. Nearly all restaurants throughout the world have early bird and "Blue Plate" specials.

46. Don't overtip if you aren't in the United States. Be aware of places where the tip is already included or not expected. Ask locals for advice if you aren't sure what to tip.

47. To save money at restaurants if there are two of you traveling, have one order a side salad and another order an entree.

48. Always get the most out of public transit. Often a single ticket will work for round-trips, transfers and an hour of travel. Day passes are often the cheapest.

49. Consider museum or event passes to save time and money. Often you can get a pass that saves you money if you can fit multiple stops within a couple of days.

50. If you get sick while traveling it is best to see a doctor sooner rather than later. Depending on where you travel, a clinic can be cheaper than waiting until you get home. Talk to your hotel to get pointed in the right direction.

These tips will help you travel for cheap. But you won't be traveling all the time. So let's look at a few more ways you can save money at home on everyday things like cleaning and health.

5 ORGANIC WAYS TO SAVE ON CLEANING PRODUCTS

Whether you want to live frugally or you simply want to eliminate or reduce the toxicity in your life, plant-based products can be a great way to clean your home. Consider the following five organic ways to make your own cleaning products.

SALT

Half a cup of salt poured down a clogged drain will have a sandblasting effect on built up scum. After pouring the salt down the drain, run warm water for a few minutes to help it work its way through the system.

A teaspoon of salt will remove grease from pans. Sprinkle liberally over the pan and then follow with a clean wet sponge or rag.

Sprinkling salt on hot over food spills will help scrape away any food and the spill. Allow it to simmer for a few minutes and then scrape away, followed by a wet washcloth.

VINEGAR

Vinegar and an old toothbrush can whiten grout. Dip the toothbrush in vinegar and work it over the grout until stains lift. Wipe away the dirt and mold and repeat until it turns white again.

A bowl of vinegar in the microwave until it boils will absorb remaining odors in the kitchen when left on the counter. You can also pour vinegar into a pan and allow it to simmer on the stove.

Fill a kettle halfway with vinegar and allow it to come to a boil. Leave overnight and then rinse to remove stains. Pour vinegar into the coffee maker and then run it through the system to remove stains.

BAKING SODA

Use baking soda to eliminate tea or coffee mug stains. Fill the mug with one part baking soda and two parts water. Allow to soak overnight, then rub clean the next day.

Add a half cup of baking soda to the laundry detergent. Run a normal cycle to help remove stains and brighten the laundry.

LEMON

Rub half a lemon over stained doors or sinks to remove hard water stains. Follow with a squeegee for extra shine.

Run your hands with lemon juice and water to remove tough smells like garlic, onions or some meats.

Add a few drops of lemon juice to dish soap in order to increase its grease fighting properties.

A drop of olive oil on a clean, cotton cloth will shine shoes. Literally a drop is all that is needed.

A few drops of olive oil and a little elbow grease will remove stickers and price tags. However, this may stain cardboard items.

A soft cotton cloth and a few drops of olive oil will polish and shine metal.

In addition to using natural remedies to clean your home, it is also possible to use natural products to help make beauty products for use by your family to save money.

7 INGREDIENTS FOR HOMEMADE ORGANIC BEAUTY PRODUCTS

In addition to making your own cleaning products, you can make your own organic beauty products. This can not only save you some money, but it can also be a healthier alternative to the popular chemical products sold on the market today. Let's consider seven essential ingredients you should keep around the house and the products you can make with them.

COCONUT OIL

Coconut oil can be used to cook and by itself it makes an excellent skin lotion. Unrefined, organic coconut oil does well for cooking, but a cheaper expeller pressed oil could be used in skin recipes to save more money.

SHEA BUTTER

After coconut oil, this is the second most commonly used natural beauty ingredient. Organic, unrefined shea butter has a natural nutty, earthy smell that is very mild. Shea butter is very nourishing for the skin, in fact, is has been known to help improve eczema.

In addition, shea butter has natural antibacterial properties so it can be used for stretch marks, wound healing and an anti-aging skin treatment. It has a natural SPF of about five so it can be used as a daily sunscreen. Some products you can made from shea butter include lotion, lotion bars, deodorant, face cream, baby lotion, diaper cream and others.

COCOA BUTTER

This can be a great addition to natural beauty recipes. It offers the added benefit of a delicate chocolate scent. Consider mixing it with mint or citrus essential oils for lotion bars and lotion or face cream.

BEESWAX

This is a natural thickening agent, and the high-quality versions have a gentle honey sent. It can be used in lotions, lotion bars, baby care recipes, lip balm, foot cream and lots of other recipes. Only a little is needed for most recipes, and just a pound will last for six months or more depending on how much you make from it.

LIQUID CARRIER OIL

If you want a smoother lotion, baby oil, salves or after-shave balms, then you need to have something thinner than coconut oil or butter. This is where liquid carrier oil comes into play. The most popular options are olive oil, almond oil, and apricot kernel oil. Apricot kernel oil offers you the most gentle scent, and almond oil is relatively unscented. However, olive oil is going to be your cheapest option if you don't mind the olive scent in your recipes. This shouldn't be a problem is you are going to add essential oils for scent.

ARROWROOT POWDER

Arrowroot is a great thickening option for sauces when cooking, but it can also be added to natural recipes such as deodorant, baby powder, diaper cream, dry shampoo and other similar recipes. It is similar to cornstarch and can also be used in a lot of makeup recipes.

ESSENTIAL OILS

While essential oils aren't really necessary for beauty products you make at home, they can provide a great range of natural scents. Some of the more popular scents include mint, lavender, lemon, orange, and sandalwood.

These are the seven most important ingredients to have on hand. Depending on the specific natural beauty products you need at home you can look up a specific recipe that tells you how much of each ingredient you need to make your product.

HERBAL REMEDIES FOR COMMON AILMENTS

When you start growing your home garden for food, also consider planting an herb garden. Herbs not only flavor your food, but they can be used as first aid and treatment for a range of common ailments. Herbs for medicinal purposes offer a natural and safe remedy. Let's take a look at the various herbs and the common ailments they treat.

- Acne - Calendula, aloe, tea tree.

- Allergy - Chamomile.

- Angina - Hawthorn, garlic, willow, green tea.

- Anxiety and Stress - Hops, kava, passionflower, valerian, chamomile, lavender

- Arthritis - Capsicum, ginger, turmeric, willow, cat's claw, devil's claw

- Athlete's Foot - Topical tea tree oil

- Boils - Tea tree oil, topical garlic, echinacea, ginseng, Eleutherococcus

- Bronchitis - Echinacea, pelargonium

- Burns - Aloe

- Cankers - Goldenseal

- Colds - Echinacea, ginseng, coffee, licorice root and tea

- Constipation - Apple, psyllium seed, senna

- Cough - Eucalyptus

- Depression - St. John's wort

- Diarrhea - Bilberry, Raspberry

- Diverticulitis - Peppermint

- Dizziness - Ginger, Ginkgo

- Earache - Echinacea

- Eczema - Chamomile, topical borage seed oil, evening primrose oil

- Flu - Echinacea, elderberry syrup

- Gas - Fennel, dill

- Gingivitis - Goldenseal, green tea

- Hay Fever - Stinging nettle, butterbur

- High Blood Pressure - Garlic, beans, cocoa, hawthorn

- High Cholesterol - Apple, cinnamon, cocoa, evening primrose oil, flaxseed, soy foods, green tea

- Hot Flashes - Red clover, soy, black cohosh

- Indigestion - Chamomile, ginger, peppermint

- Infection - Topical tea tree oil, astragalus, echinacea, Eleutherococcus, garlic, ginseng

- Insomnia - Kava, evening primrose, hops, lemon balm, valerian

- Irregularity - Senna, Psyllium seed

- Irritable Bowel Syndrome - Chamomile, peppermint

- Lower back pain - Thymol, carvacrol, white willow bark

- Menstrual cramps - Kava, raspberry

- Migraine - Feverfew, butterbur

- Morning sickness - Ginger

- Muscle pain - Capsicum, wintergreen

- Nausea - Ginger

- Shingles - Capsicum

- Sore throat - Licorice, marshmallow, mullein

- Stuffy nose - Echinacea

- Toothache - Willow, clove oil

- Ulcers - Aloe, Licorice

- Yeast infection - Garlic, Goldenseal

It is easy to see how herbs can be used to treat pretty much anything. However, it is important to talk to your doctor before taking any herbs; especially if you are already taking other medications.

HOW TO FIND FREE STUFF: ONLINE AND OFFLINE

Both online and offline there are hundreds of items you can get for free. There are a few tricks and tips you need to employ in order to get these deals and enjoy free stuff. Let's take a moment to consider both online and offline free stuff individually to see how you can get things for free.

SEARCHING

The best place to start your search is with the many sites that distribute free stuff. If you aren't looking for anything specific, then you can just try typing "free stuff" into your search box and see what comes up in the results.

You will likely come across many websites that are devoted to giving away high ticket items such as iPods, computers or game systems. It can be difficult to determine which of these websites is legit. Sometimes it is best to go through a website that rates various free websites or a forum that allows you to discuss free offers with others to see what has worked and what hasn't.

If you are looking for a specific free item, but can't find it, then you can try a search engine. Enter the item you are looking for in the search box along with the word free. If you don't get any decent results, then enter the term "+ free" and enclose your phrase in quotation marks to limits your results to the specific phrase.

For your local area, you can use community-based sites such as Freecycle, Craigslist, and Nextdoor to help you find people offering free stuff in your community.

GETTING FREE SAMPLES

Mailing Lists

When you sign up for mailing lists, you will often get free promotions. If you want a free sample of a new product or you have a favorite company or retailer you want to get the newest releases from then your best option is to sign up for the mailing list. Often you get free coupons or codes that allow you to redeem the free sample.

Online Surveys

Most companies know the value of consumer data, and they are willing to get it by giving away prizes or cash compensation. If you take an online survey, it may take a little of your time, but you will get free stuff in the end.

Coupons

Keep an eye on weekly mailers from grocery stores, retail stores, and other places in order to get buy one get one or completely free coupons. Clip these coupons and keep them separate with expiration dates so you can get as much free stuff as possible. A lot of stores will do this to market new products to customers.

Complain

Although not the ideal option, but if you straight-up complain to a person in charge you can often get free stuff. Often the best interest of a retail manager is to just offer free stuff to get a problem to go away rather than reason with customers or offer refunds. If you're willing to complain to someone, you will stand a decent chance of getting something for free.

Just remember that you need to have a good reason for why the product is unacceptable. Simply stating you didn't like it or it didn't fit isn't going to be a good enough reason. If you are in a store, ask to speak with the manager. If you bring a product home, then call the customer service number or the store.

Ask

If you're at a store and want to try food, perfume or other product before purchasing, most retailers will be happy to provide you with samples. Find a salesperson and let them know about your interest and ask to try a sample. Most stores will provide you with a sample if you just ask. Just because you receive a sample doesn't mean you are under obligation to purchase the item.

GETTING FREE FOOD

Free Coffee

You will be surprised at some of the places you can get free food and drink. For example, many big banks offer free coffee in the lobby. More obviously, if you sign up for a free rewards program through coffee stores such as Starbucks, Dunkin' Donuts, and Caribou Coffee, you will be able to get free coffee.

Continental Breakfast

This is another situation that isn't ideal and requires some acting on your part. If there is a hotel chain in your area with a continental breakfast room, this can be an option. This isn't illegal, but if problems arise just leave quietly.

Farmer's Market

At most farmer's markets, the vendors want to get rid of everything before they pack up and head home. If you approach a booth ten to fifteen minutes before the close of the day, you can often get a decent deal. Ask about their 'two for one' deals or whether they have over-ripe stuff they want to get rid of.

Street Festivals

At these events, most vendors are offering free samples in order to hook passers-by. You can often get free food, free products and a lot of other stuff as well.

Free Tastes

At most retail locations you can get samples of wine, beer, chocolate, fresh produce and other goods. This is because the sellers are hoping you will like a product so much you are willing to pay the price for it.

Dumpster Diving

If this is legal in your area and you don't mind a little dirty work, you will be surprised what you may find. Go behind a grocery store, restaurant or other food outlets. You can often find out of date canned good, bruised produce or any other variety of items deemed unsellable.

Forage

If you enjoy nature walks as a way to get your frugal entertainment, you can combine it with foraging to get free food. Learn to recognize the edible plants in your area and then, while you're out hiking, you can get greens, berries, and nuts. Once you get home, wash thoroughly, and you're good to go.

GETTING FREE ENTERTAINMENT

Free Internet

If you aren't a heavy internet user, then paying for it may be too costly. The easier option is to use coffee shops, retail locations and other free internet spots to do your online work.

Free Newspapers

Not many people pay for newspaper subscriptions anymore since they can get it for free online. You can often get free newspapers at college campuses. Also, most larger towns have free weeklies that focus on niche markets, and you can find them around coffee shops, bookstores, and other local venues.

Visit the Library

The best place to get free entertainment is the library. Here you can use the internet for free, read the newspaper, check out books, DVDs, and CDs. Just make sure you return everything on time, and you'll have a completely free resource.

Free Music

Downloading music for free isn't always illegal. Often new groups or new sounds will offer music for free to get people interested. There are websites such as Bandcamp, Soundcloud, and Noise Trade that offer free singles, downloads, and whole albums. Some do have a 'pay what you want' plan so if you really like the artist and their music, you can leave a few dollars if you choose to do so.

Public TV

Depending on how much TV you watch, it can be cheaper to cancel your cable plan and just watch TV in public. If you only want to watch sports, consider heading to the local bar. Or you can go to the library and watch shows for free on the internet.

Go at Closing Time

This may not be the most reliable option, but sometimes if you show up to an event close to closing, you may be able to get in for free or at the least at a discounted price. Better yet, if the concert is outdoors you don't even have to pay to go in; just set up on the outside and you get a free concert.

It is easy to see how you can get a lot of free stuff with just a little bit of work. Next, let's take a look at how you can establish a budget to help you save money, so you have more to work with.

Exactly how much you may save by living a frugal lifestyle will depend on how many of the tips in this book you implement. However, I can give you an example of how much I saved to help give you some inspiration to start your own frugal living.

When it comes to purchasing food the average American family spends between $3,500-$5,000 a year according to statistics. We spent $1,900 after growing most of my own food at home. This is a savings of $3,100 a year!

By implementing home improvement and utility savings listed above we only spent about $1,750 while the average US household spent $5,521. A savings of $3,771 a year!

On gas and transportation, we spent about $1583 a year while the average is $5,755. A savings of $4,172!

For entertainment, we spent about $100 while the average is $1,029, a savings of $929.

This is just on the four major areas alone. In total, we have saved $11,972 a year compared to any other average family. That is a huge chunk of money to have back in your wallet. And this is just on the big four areas alone. I'm not talking about the savings we get from doing small projects around the home, so we don't have to buy everyday items at the store or saving money on things like a vacation.

Housing	Expenses
Mortgage or rent	$1,241
Phones(2)	$75
Electricity	$91
Gas	$27
Water and sewer	$25
Cable/Internet	$0
Maintenance or repairs	$0
Supplies	$0
Other	$0
Subtotals	$1,494

Transportation

Car Note	$0
Health Insurance	$287
Auto Insurance	$129

Licensing	$0
Fuel	$141
Maintenance	$18
Other	$0
Subtotals	$675

Food

Groceries	$177
Dining out	$39
Dog Food	$24
Subtotals	$340

Personal Care

Medical(Co-pay & Prescription)	$128
Hair/nails	$18
Clothing	$35
Dry cleaning	$0
Health club	$0
Organization dues or fees	$0
Movies, games, DVDs	$10
Subtotals	$191

Loans

Personal (Medical Loan)	$0
Credit card - Chase	$59
Credit card - Discover	$0
Credit card - Citi	$75
Other	$0
Subtotals	$134

All Total Expenses	**$2,599**

Income

Income David	$3,675.00
Income Joyce	$1,150.00
Total Income:	$4,825.00
Net Savings (Loss)	$2,225.74

Let's look at first expense report I showed you at the beginning of this book, if you compare these two, you will see that our income stayed almost the same but only difference is that our expenses have gone down from $5,424 to $2,599, that is a savings of $2,825!! That is a huge savings, I am sure you will agree.

Now let me tell you a few other details that I have not yet mentioned. When you look at both of my expense charts side by side, you will see that the huge medical related loan that I took out for Joyce is now gone, I paid it off. How? I will get to it in a second, but let's also take a note that along with what I mentioned above about the big four savings, we are also paying less on credit card bills to. Did you notice that?

Okay, I am sure you are wondering how I was able to pay off such a big loan and how we are paying less on our credit card payments. We shopped around and found a good mortgage company locally and refinanced our home for a lower rate and while doing that we were able to take some equity from the house, and thus paid off that loan and paid down on the 3 credit cards also.

So you see frugal living is not about cutting down on grocery bills or shopping for pre-owned clothing, but about smart personal financial planning as well.

Hopefully, these numbers have inspired you to start your own frugal lifestyle. Even if you aren't ready to just dive into the entire frugal lifestyle yet, let me take a moment also to show you how you can get things for free.

HOW TO CREATE A BUDGET NO MATTER WHAT YOUR INCOME AND SAVE 25% A MONTH

A budget had a huge impact on your financial life. It can help you get rid of outstanding debt, change your financial future and even improve your mental and physical health. Depending on your situation, developing a budget doesn't necessarily mean spending less; rather it may just mean you need to make more effective financial decisions. Joyce started doing our family budget, and since she started, we noticed it is fun to race every month to see if we are below our target or over, and often we find ourselves being below the budget and then we take the kids out for a good treat. It is really fun.

Let's consider how you can develop a budget.

TRACKING INCOME AND EXPENSES

In order to start tracking your spending history, you need to collect all your past bills, bank and credit card statements and receipts. This way you can put together an accurate estimate of how much you spend in a month.

If you aren't good with finance, then you may want to consider using software to help you with your budget. Most of these programs have built-in budget making tools that will help you customize your budget along with analytics that help you project where your cash will go in the future and better understand your spending habits. Some good choices for this software include Mint, Quicken, Microsoft Money, AceMoney, and BudgetPulse. If your PC has Microsoft Office installed on it, then just open up Excel, and you will see some free personal budget templates there, you can't beat the price; it is free.

If you're going to do it yourself, then you want to create a spreadsheet. The goal is to chart all your expenses and income over the course of a year. The spreadsheet should clearly show all of your information so you can quickly identify areas where you need to spend smarter.

Add up all of your expenses and revenues for the last 12 months using your bank and credit card data. If you're on a fixed salary, then you know how much you bring home every week. If you have a salary that varies each month, you can get an accurate view of your average monthly revenue by documenting a year's history.

If you work for yourself, then keep in mind that what you are bringing home isn't the same as what you earn. Figure out how much you are likely to pay in taxes and subtract that from your monthly income to get an accurate number.

Next, add all of your monthly expenses on the spreadsheet. Consider the bills you have to pay every month. Average how much you spend every week on gasoline or groceries. How much do you spend on eating out or entertainment? When you track a year of actual spending, you will get an accurate view of your spending habits. I was surprised at how much I underestimated the amount I thought I was spending every month.

Now you need to analyze your revenue and expenses. If you find your expenses are greater than your revenue, you are living beyond your means. You will then need to divide your budget into one of two groups.

Fixed expenses are things that happen every month like bills, insurance, loan debts, food and necessary shopping items such as household products and clothing.

Discretionary expenses are unfixed expenses that are optional. This includes savings, entertainment, vacation funds and other such luxuries.

CREATING A BUDGET

The information you gained from tracking revenue and expenses will help you create an accurate preliminary budget. The first step is to calculate your fixed expenses and revenue, then determine how you are going to spend your discretionary money.

To calculate fixed expenses, take an average for each month over the past year and then add 5%. Be sure to account for changes to fixed expenses, such as adding payments for a new car or paying off a loan.

The next step is to set goals for the bulk of your discretionary spending. Once you know how much leftover money you should have at the end of the month, determine how you want to spend it. The goal you set should be clear, explicit and actionable.

Perhaps it is setting a specific amount aside into the savings, pay off a credit card faster or set aside a specific amount for a vacation.

There are ways that you can save money and get tax benefits. If you put money directly from your paycheck into a 401(K) or personal IRA, the money can be deducted before it is subject to taxes. Some companies will even do partial matching so you can make your savings go even further.

When you budget out your discretionary spending, your focus should be on values. What are your values and how do you want to spend your money in order to realize them? Most people choose to spend money on hobbies, interests or charities. Think of it as investing in an experience or a feeling of satisfaction. You want to spend your money on something that is going to make you happy

BECOME AN EXPERT AT BUDGETING

After you have set a budget, it is important to stick to it and don't overspend. This is the first and most important rule of budgeting. It may seem obvious, but you will be surprised at how easy it is to go over budget even when you have one clearly in place. Be watchful of your spending habits and know where your money is going.

Larger expenses are always unpleasant, but the most effective ways to deal with them are by staying within a budget. If you take a vacation every year, consider staying home one time.

Although smaller expenses can add up as well so you need to do what you can to reduce them. Cut back on the frequency of expensive luxuries. Switch to generic brands. A lot of what I already discussed in this book can help you reduce your smaller expenses and save you money.

It is important to treat yourself occasionally, but keep it within reason. Your money should work for you and not the other way around; you don't want to be a slave to your budget. At least once a month, treat yourself to something that won't break the budget. However, don't let your rewards system become counterproductive to the point that it affects your budget. When you treat yourself to something small, you will be less likely to splurge on a more expensive item.

Ideally, you should get to the point where you have no credit card debt and avoid using credit cards if at all possible. However, if you are going to use credit cards for purchases try to keep them at a zero balance each month to avoid additional fees. If you can't pay off the current balances, set up a reasonable time period for paying them off so you can get back to a zero balance.

For most weekly purchases, you should switch to paying cash for them. This is especially true for any extras such as eating out at a restaurant. This will help you control spending since you are more aware when paying with cash rather than with a card.

When you file your taxes, you can often have a better advantage with itemized deductions. Start keeping receipts, especially if you are a self-employed individual. There are many things you can consider as expenses when doing your taxes as a self-employed individual.

Lastly, when budgeting your money, don't rely on windfalls. A lot of time people will factor in money that they aren't sure they will be getting. This includes year-end bonuses, inheritances or tax refunds. When you are setting up a budget, you should only include guaranteed money.

Now that you have budgeted and set aside money, you can start investing to help your money grow and go further. Consider how your savings can grow and save you, even more money.

HOW TO GROW YOUR SAVINGS BY INVESTING

Frugal living and budgeting are going to help put money back in your pocket. While it may be tempting to use this money to buy something you've always wanted or to take a nice, long vacation; why not consider growing these savings by investing that extra money? This way you can have a good retirement, or you can have a strong emergency fund should something unforeseen happen. Let's take a look at how investing can help you grow your savings.

Before investing there are three rules you need to be aware of:

1. Higher the risk, higher the returns. There is always a risk, however minimal.

2. There are no free gifts. If something sounds too good to be true, it probably is.

3. Never underestimate the power of compounding.

WHY INVEST

The simplest reason for investing is because money loses value over time. If you were to buy a product today that you bought five years ago, you would get a much less quantity today for the same amount. This is because of inflation. Since you can't avoid inflation, then you need to grow your money over time as its value lessens.

If you invest wisely and let the power of compounding multiply, then you will increase your hard earned income and have a little extra to spend. It is important to start early. The earlier you start, the faster you will gain rewards. However, it is never too late to begin. If you have money you don't need urgently, then consider investing it.

However, before investing it is important to ask yourself why you're investing. You need a financial goal, such as repaying a loan or a future expense. When you define a financial goal, you will be able to decide how much to invest and how long you need to stay invested. This will then help you determine your risk appetite or how much you are willing to risk.

Risk Appetite

Risk appetite is defined as the amount and type of risk that a person is willing to take in order to reach their objectives. You should have a realistic understanding of your ability and willingness to deal with large swings in the value or your investments. This will also help you determine which investment options you finally go ahead with based on your risk profile.

Expected Rate of Return

Before considering other things you always want to find out what you stand to gain. Expected return is the amount one expects to get from an investment. A simple option is to just Google the expected return on the investment option you are considering.

This will tell you how much you can gain if you invest in that option or asset. You can then compare it to your goal and target duration. This shows you how much you are going to need to invest in order to get the targeted amount in the targeted time frame.

Risk Profile

By now you've determined your financial goal and the expected rate of return of various investment options to find out how much you need to invest. Now you need to determine how risky the various options are so you can determine which is the best for you to invest in to grow your savings.

There are independent rating agencies throughout the world such as S&P, Moodys and others that will rate financial instruments based on complex models. They will also provide you with a detailed analysis of current trends. Globally these agencies are trusted by all. Check their opinions before you invest in anything.

Tax Exemptions

Another factor to consider before investing your money is the exemption on taxes because it has an impact on the overall return on your investment. An investment option with a lower rate of return will give you a better value if you take into consideration the amount you save in taxes.

Using this framework you can carefully consider all of your investment options and make the right choice. Once you've finished, you will be ready to make an informed decision about how to invest your savings. However, make sure you read all the fine print before you invest. Make sure you understand all of the terms and conditions clearly so you can avoid any surprises later on in the process.

CONCLUSION

Now that you've finished this book we hope you have realized the benefits you can gain from frugal living and realize that it isn't as difficult as you may have thought. We have learned that frugal living is about so much more than simply improving one's financial situation.

When we started living frugally, we noticed how the life became simpler slowly. A simpler life has changed our experience of the world and has improved our emotional, physical and mental health.

We have also learned to be more artful. Now when I look at things, I think of all the possibilities. This means we are always looking for ways to make our life better and we are much more aware of how little we really need to be happy.

Frugal living also benefits the environment since it is a green living option. Now that I'm living frugally, I'm not wasting as much. I feel good about not only saving money but protecting the environment as well.

Perhaps the best thing about frugal living is the amount of free time it opens up for you. I'm working less and spending more time with my family and doing things we actually care about, including myself. I'm able to spend some time for myself and work on my hobbies. This goes a long way to improving my overall health.

So take all this into consideration and see whether frugal living is for you. I promise you won't be disappointed at the benefits you will enjoy.

Appendix

101 SMART MONEY SAVING TIPS

GROCERY, COOKING & EATING:

1. Keep a price book of per unit food costs.

2. Purchase based on unit costs to get the best deal.

3. Try cheaper store brands.

4. Never go to the grocery store hungry.

5. Don't use vending machines.

6. Always travel with a snack and bottle of water.

7. Reduce or eliminate consumable habits such as smoking and alcohol.

CARS AND FUEL:

8. Shop around for insurance.

9. Ask your city about car share programs.

10. Change your own oil and other basic maintenance.

11. Avoid buying premium gas.

12. Look for discounts for on-board monitoring equipment.

13. Do any auto repairs you can teach yourself.

14. Opt for high insurance deductibles.

UTILITIES:

15. Let dishes air dry.

16. Take shorter showers.

17. Turn off your PC when not using it.

18. During cold weather use a heated mattress pad.

19. Use a small space heater in a room you close off.

20. Plug appliances into power strips and turn off when not using them.

21. Adjust your computer's power settings to power down or sleep after inactivity.

22. Shut vents and close doors in unused rooms.

MEDICAL NEEDS:

23. Use a flexible spending account for out-of-pocket medical expenses.

24. Ask your doctor to prescribe generic medication.

25. Buy generic medications at a discount pharmacy.

26. Ask a doctor or dentist if they have sliding-scale fees.

27. Look for free and low-cost clinics.

28. Go online to GoodRx to get the lowest price for prescriptions.

SCHOOL NEEDS:

29. Attend a state or community college.

30. Visit FAFSA.gov for financial aid options.

31. Consider an accredited online college.

32. Consider transferring after two years.

33. Buy or rent textbooks online.

34. Watch for unique scholarship opportunities.

TECHNOLOGY:

35. Look for digital subscriptions of your magazines.

36. Use Skype for long-distance calls.

37. Research all major purchases online first.

38. Follow through on rebate offers.

39. Never buy anything over $500 without a discount or sale.

40. Avoid extended warranties.

41. Use rechargeable batteries.

42. Store batteries in the refrigerator.

PERSONAL CARE PRODUCTS:

43. Downgrade to less expensive brands.

44. Collect free samples.

45. Try it before you buy it.

46. Buy makeup that does double duty.

47. Only buy the most important and necessary products.

48. Fix broken makeup.

49. Cut your own hair.

50. Do your own manicures.

FINANCIAL:

51. Opt out of overdraft protection.

52. Switch to an online bank.

53. Avoid using ATMs.

54. Check each bank statement for errors or new fees.

55. Automate bill paying.

56. Itemize deductions on your tax return.

57. Monitor credit card interest rates.

58. Avoid credit cards with annual fees.

59. Contact credit card companies for a rate reduction.

60. Pay yourself an allowance in cash to avoid using cards.

61. Track your spending and set savings goals.

62. Avoid carrying your credit card.

63. Consider a zero percent balance transfer deal.

64. Consider balance transfer fees before moving a balance.

65. Break long-term goals into short-term goals to make them more manageable.

HOUSEHOLD:

---

66. Consolidate insurance carriers to qualify for discounts.

67. Get competing quotes on insurance once a year.

68. Check for new discounts through AAA or other organizations.

69. Before buying online, factor in shipping costs for price comparisons.

70. Factor quality into buying decisions.

71. Embrace minimalism.

72. Shop thrift stores before buying furniture.

73. Use washable rags rather than paper towels.

74. Check mortgage rates regularly for refinancing opportunities.

75. Look into refinancing if your credit history improves or home value changes.

76. Consider a shorter-term mortgage.

77. Research property taxes before you buy.

78. See if you qualify for federal tax credit for appliance purchases.

79. Research which plants naturally suit your climate.

80. Use only half a dishwasher tablet.

81. Do repairs once a week to keep things in good working order so they last longer.

82. Do home repairs yourself.

83. Reuse things.

84. Wash and re-use Ziploc bags.

85. See if a local dump offers free firewood or garden mulch.

86. Use water from boiling eggs or pasta to water plants.

87. Flush the toilet only after you use it two to three times.

88. Cancel club memberships.

89. Consider cheaper childcare options.

90. Reduce or eliminate organized child activities.

91. Move to a less expensive area.

92. Join a tool-lending library.

MISCELLANEOUS:

---

93. Use employee discounts.

94. Sell something every week.

95. Never spend change, rather put it in a savings account.

96. Get rid of excess stuff.

97. Have a garage sale.

98. If you get a raise, don't increase your lifestyle.

99. Change your mindset to what can you use and not what do you need to   buy.

100.   Find a live-in elder care position.

101.   For short-term stays, become a house sitter or pet sitter.

CPSIA information can be obtained
at www.ICGtesting.com
Printed in the USA
LVHW012237251219
641686LV00018B/2166/P